TIMBER PRESS
POCKET GUIDE TO
Bamboos

TIMBER PRESS
POCKET GUIDE TO

BAMBOOS

TED JORDAN MEREDITH

TIMBER PRESS
PORTLAND • LONDON

Frontispiece: The colorful culm leaves of *Fargesia* sp. 'Scabrida' cling for a time before dropping.

Published in 2009 by Timber Press, Inc.

The Haseltine Building
133 S.W. Second Avenue, Suite 450
Portland, Oregon 97204-3527
www.timberpress.com

2 The Quadrant
135 Salusbury Road
London NW6 6RJ
www.timberpress.co.uk

Designed by Christi Payne
Printed in China

ISBN-13: 978-0-88192-936-2

Library of Congress Cataloging-in-Publication Data

Meredith, Ted.
  Timber Press pocket guide to bamboos / Ted Jordan Meredith. -- 1st ed.
      p. cm.
  Includes bibliographical references and index.
  ISBN 978-0-88192-936-2
  1. Bamboo--Handbooks, manuals, etc. I. Title. II. Title: Pocket guide to bamboos.
  SB413.B2M478 2009
  635.9'349--dc22
                        2009005847

A catalog record for this book is also available from the British Library.

Acknowledgments

My thanks once again to everyone mentioned in *Bamboo for Gardens* on which this pocket guide is based, and to the vibrant community of bamboo enthusiasts and advocates around the world who continue to generously share their knowledge and insight in person and via the Internet.

The task of acquiring nearly 200 new photographs for this pocket guide within tight publishing deadlines was both daunting and joyful. Special thanks to Ned Jaquith of Bamboo Garden nursery, and Noah Bell and crew; and to Gib and Diane Cooper of Tradewinds Bamboo Nursery. Their wonderful assistance helped make this possible.

About This Book

The entries in this pocket guide are arranged in alphabetical order by scientific name. Cultivar names are enclosed by single quotation marks. Many bamboo botanical names have changed and are continuing to change as bamboo taxonomy evolves and becomes better defined.

The maximum heights and diameters listed in this book represent what is possible for bamboo in a large mature grove under ideal conditions. In most instances, a small grove in a typical landscaping situation will grow to a height in the lower to middle of the range listed.

The USDA hardiness zones offer a rough guide for the lowest zones recommended for a bamboo; however, bamboos exposed to extended periods of cold and drying in their lowest rated climate zone may still suffer winter damage. If one is willing to accept some winter damage, bamboos can sometimes be grown in zones lower than those listed.

Winter hardiness is not the only consideration when choosing bamboo. Some of the hardier subtropical bamboos will grow in temperate climates, but without sufficient summer heat may be substantially smaller and less vigorous. Conversely, montane bamboos from the Himalayas and Central and South America are generally ill suited to summer climates with hot nights and warm soils, such as those typical of the U.S. Southeast. Consult the genera and species entries in the A to Z section of this book for more detail.

The nomenclature in this book generally follows provisions of the International Code of Botanical Nomenclature (ICBN) and the International Code of Nomenclature for Cultivated Plants (ICNCP). Cultivar names are used in place of botanical *forma*, however, in accord with the convention of the American Bamboo Society (ABS).

The ABS has adapted this convention because the relative level of botanical distinction between *forma* in wild bamboo plants and that of cultivars in cultivated plants is essentially the same, and because the distinction and origins of forms evolving in the wild from those arising in cultivation is not always evident, particularly when the forms may spontaneously arise in multiple instances.

In lieu of an alternative unfamiliar cultivar name, Latin names have been used as cultivar names when the Latin name has been in common usage. For example, *Sinobambusa tootsik* f. *albostriata* is rendered *Sinobambusa tootsik* 'Albostriata'.

CONTENTS

Introduction   9

Bamboos for Specific Purposes and Locations   27

Bamboos A–Z   33

Nursery Sources   195

Glossary   200

Further Reading   203

Index   204

Opposite: In a mature grove of the giant timber bamboo *Phyllostachys vivax*, broad leaves form a tropical-looking canopy high above smooth, bright green culms. Note the white band below many of the culm nodes, a characteristic of this species.

INTRODUCTION

It is startling to think that giant timber bamboos, up to 1 ft. (30 cm) in diameter and more than 100 ft. (30 m) tall with structural properties that compare favorably with steel, have any kinship with the fine, velvety mat of the suburban putting green—but they do. Like the putting green lawn, bamboo is a grass.

Some 1400 species of bamboos are distributed throughout the world's temperate, tropical, and subtropical regions, growing from sea level to more than 14,000 ft. (4300 m). Some groundcover bamboos reach a height of only a few inches and can be mowed like a lawn. At the other end of the scale are timber bamboos that live up to their name, growing like timber and forming towering forests.

Except for the giant oceanic kelp, bamboo is the world's fastest-growing plant. New bamboo culms can grow more than several feet in a 24-hour period, reaching most of their full height in 30 days. It is literally possible to watch bamboo grow.

Europe and Antarctica are the only continents without indigenous populations of bamboo, yet since their introduction into Europe, bamboos have flourished in many areas from the Mediterranean to the Arctic Circle in Norway. Not unexpectedly, the bamboos that are native to tropical regions are highly cold sensitive and may suffer damage with only the slightest frost. At the other end of the spectrum, some species of the genus *Fargesia*, indigenous to China's mountainous regions, are among the world's hardiest bamboos, able to withstand temperatures of -20°F (-29°C) without damage.

Bamboo culms and branches are typically green, but striking color combinations are common. Culms may be yellow, brown, brick, or black, and striped in different patterns of green, yellow, brown, and black, or mottled with brown

or black. Yellow culms may sometimes turn red when exposed to sun and cold. Young culms of many species are coated with a waxy powder that is manifest in various tones of blue. New culm sheaths exhibit striking color and pattern variations.

A shrub-sized mound of *Pleioblastus pygmaeus* (foreground) complements the arborescent timber bamboo *Phyllostachys viridis* 'Robert Young' (background).

Opposite: Along this pond, *Phyllostachys atrovaginata* creates a shaded respite and integrates seamlessly with trees, shrubs, and indigenous vegetation.

Culms of *Phyllostachys viridis* 'Robert Young' change color with age.

Leaf sizes range from tiny with an Asiatic delicacy to 2 ft. (60 cm) in length with a lush tropical look. Leaf colors range from light green to deep green and numerous variegated patterns with tones of yellow, gold, apricot, cream, and white. Bamboo's beauty, and its diversity in size, texture, and color, offer the landscaper and gardener an abundant palette.

Growth Habits

Grasses, including bamboos, are characterized by a jointed stem called a culm. Leaves or branches emerge alternately, at the joints, in two ranks along the stem. The leaves consist of a leaf sheath surrounding the culm or branch, and a leaf blade growing free of the culm or branch.

The culms are typically hollow, but they can be solid. Each culm section starts and ends with a solid joint called a node. Nodes are usually visible as a swelling encircling the culm. The sections between the nodes are called internodes. The culms of most grasses have high silica content and are shiny.

These aforementioned features are characteristic of all grasses. In the case of the giant timber bamboos, we see the typical grass characteristics played out on a grand scale..

Bamboo has a different growth habit than most plants in the garden. Understanding how bamboo grows is key to making the best use of it in the landscape and maintaining it within desired boundaries.

We have mentioned that bamboos have aboveground stems called culms. Bamboos also have underground stems called rhizomes. There are essentially two types of bamboo rhizomes, pachymorph and leptomorph. Bamboo rhizome types have a bearing on how bamboo grows and how we control its spread, so let us briefly examine the characteristics of the two rhizomes.

A **pachymorph rhizome** always turns upward and becomes a culm. It is nearly always curved and, at its maximum width, is slightly thicker than the aboveground culm it becomes. New rhizomes emerge from buds on an existing rhizome. As with the original rhizome, these new rhizomes always turn upward and become culms.

Pachymorph rhizomes are generally associated with clumping bamboos. For practical purposes, for most bamboos with pachymorph rhizomes suitable for North American and European climates, this is the case.

Most bamboos with pachymorph rhizomes are either tropical or semitropical, but some of the hardiest bamboos, such as species of the aforementioned genus *Fargesia*, have pachymorph rhizomes and a clumping habit

A **leptomorph rhizome** runs laterally underground and usually does not turn upward to become a culm. A leptomorph rhizome is smaller in diameter than the culms that originate from it. Most buds remain dormant, but those that germinate may produce either culms or new rhizomes. The new rhizomes also run laterally underground and generate more new culms and more new rhizomes.

The pachymorph rhizome of a clumping bamboo always turns upward to form a culm.

The leptomorph rhizome of a running bamboo. A new culm is initiating at one of the nodes. New rhizomes can also initiate along its length.

Leptomorph rhizomes are generally associated with running bamboos and temperate-climate growing regions. Bamboos with leptomorph rhizomes generally require measures to control their spread and restrict them to desired areas. We will discuss these methods in the next section, "Controlling Spread."

Bamboos with leptomorph rhizomes have two pronounced growth periods, one period of aboveground growth for the culms, occurring in spring through early summer for most bamboos, and another period of underground growth for the rhizomes, in late summer through the fall for most bamboos.

The period of aboveground growth is quite dramatic, and after a dreary winter, an emphatic affirmation of life, vigor, and vitality. Emerging from the ground at the full diameter of the new culm, new shoots thrust skyward at an astonishing rate, achieving up to 90 percent of their full height in 30 days.

So, what does this mean? This means that if you have a bamboo approximately 3 ft. (90 cm) tall, a new shoot will emerge to form a new culm and achieve approximately 90 percent of that 3-ft. height in 30 days. This also means that if you have a bamboo three stories tall, a new

culm will achieve approximately 90 percent of that three-story-tall height in 30 days.

In an established grove, timber bamboo can grow more than 3 ft. in a 24-hour period. Even in a suburban plot, growth of 1 ft. (30 cm) a day for timber bamboo is not uncommon. Needless to say, the rapid growth of a bamboo can be stunningly dramatic.

As the dramatic period of aboveground growth is completed, the rhizomes of leptomorph bamboos begin a period of underground growth and initiate new rhizomes from buds on the existing rhizomes. The underground growth of the new rhizomes can be quite vigorous and extend in multiple directions. This is the growth habit that gives running bamboo its name.

Bamboos with pachymorph rhizomes are similarly dramatic in their growth, although the growth of the new culms may be extended over a somewhat longer period. Unlike leptomorph bamboos, the rhizomes of pachymorph bamboos always turn upward to become culms, and thus they do not have a network of underground rhizomes or an overtly distinct period of rhizome growth.

As a new bamboo shoot elongates, it forms a new culm and generates branches and leaves. In succeeding years, the culm never grows any taller or increases in diameter. In a developing grove, however, the new culms in the following year will be larger in diameter and taller, sometimes by nearly a factor of two. Bamboo can rapidly develop an evergreen screen, hedge, or specimen plant for the garden.

Controlling Spread

Most pachymorph bamboos that are suitable for North American and European climates have rhizomes with short necks and a clumping habit. These bamboos expand slowly around their perimeter from year to year, maintaining a generally

The delicate, temperate-climate *Fargesia nitida* is an example of a clumping bamboo. No special measures are needed to contain its growth.

Clumping bamboos as well as running bamboos can make an effective privacy screen. Here a young plant of *Thamnocalamus crassinodus* 'Aristatus' begins to form a screen and barrier along the street. A number of plants will effectively form a hedge.

At the other end of the size scale, the giant tropical bamboo, *Dendrocalamus giganteus*, is also tightly clumping.

symmetrical shape of the clump. If the perimeter is becoming too large, spread can be controlled by simply removing the culms at the perimeter with a saw, or snapping off the new shoots as they emerge from the ground.

A few pachymorph bamboos with somewhat elongated rhizome necks, such as species of the genus *Yushania*, do grow well in North American and European climates. For control purposes, they can be treated like running bamboos, though in many soils and climates many behave more like clumpers with a somewhat more open culm spacing.

Running bamboos behave in a manner largely unfamiliar to American and European cultures. Mentioning bamboo in a gathering of any size is nearly certain to prompt hysterical cursing from someone who has experienced an attack from the demonic plant that invaded unexpectedly and ceaselessly, and could not be stopped or killed. In North America and Europe, running bamboos primarily equate to temperate-climate bamboos with leptomorph rhizomes.

Without intervention, a newly planted running bamboo may send up new culms in a relatively close clump for perhaps a year or two, giving the impression of a benign growth habit. Then, suddenly one spring, new culms may emerge many feet away from the original plant. In subsequent years, the bamboo will make additional leaps, as the now much larger plant further extends itself in proportion to its much larger size and greater vigor. By this time, bamboo is unexpectedly coming up everywhere, and the invasion is in full swing—surely a sad tale, but it doesn't have to be this way. The spread of running bamboos is easily controlled as long as one understands its growth habits and applies appropriate methods.

Let us now examine the growth habit of running rhizomes in more detail. We have mentioned that running bamboos with leptomorph rhizomes have two major growth periods, one of the aboveground growth of new culms, and another of the underground growth of new rhizomes. Unlike older woody rhizomes, the new rhizomes are tender and can easily be severed

with a spade. And, lacking an extensive root system, the severed new rhizomes can easily be pulled from the ground. Unless turned downward by an obstacle, the new rhizomes of most species grow within the first foot (30 cm) or so of soil, and typically within the first 4 to 6 in. (10 to 15 cm) of soil.

Now that we have an understanding about how running bamboos with leptomorph rhizomes grow, we can apply our knowledge to control methods. Controlling bamboo's spread and maintaining boundaries is relatively simple. A number of strategies can be employed. Each has its advantages and areas of application.

Left unchecked this running bamboo, *Phyllostachys dulcis*, has sent up new shoots some distance from the existing clump.

Rhizome Pruning

Rhizome pruning is a relatively easy, seasonal task. It is best used where the bamboo can be readily accessed on all sides. In late fall through early spring, after the rhizomes have completed their yearly period of growth, the tender new rhizomes can be pruned by plunging a sharp, flat-bottomed garden spade into the soil around the desired perimeter of the grove. Any of the severed rhizomes that have grown outside the desired perimeter can be easily pulled from the ground.

Another variation of this method calls for digging a narrow trench about 1 ft. (30 cm) deep around the desired perimeter of the grove and filling it with a loose material such as sawdust, cedar bark, wood chips, or other similar materials. Instead of plunging a spade into the soil around the perimeter, a pick or similar tool is dragged through the trench. When rhizomes are encountered, they are severed with pruning shears and pulled out of the ground.

Rhizome pruning is not much more difficult than the task of raking the leaves of deciduous trees in the fall. Nor is it that much more difficult than edging the lawn—another, more familiar grass that requires periodic maintenance to control its spread. Although the task is relatively easy, rhizome pruning is a seasonal task that must be completed each year, without fail, in order to be effective.

Rhizome Barriers

Although a rhizome barrier requires the most initial effort, it offers a nearly maintenance-free method of control, at least for a period of years. A disadvantage is that a rhizome barrier is effectively a container, and large bamboos in smaller barrier areas can become root bound. From the standpoint of the bamboo's health and vigor over an extended period of years, it is the least preferred of the methods discussed here, but is nonetheless a good choice when the other methods are not viable.

Contained by rhizome barriers, large running timber bamboos provide a tall screen along the fence line and privacy from the neighbors. Vegetables and herbs happily occupy the foreground.

Close-up of a bamboo barrier along a fence line. The top of the barrier should remain uncovered to monitor growth and prevent rhizomes from escaping over the top.

Where a grove borders an inaccessible area, such as a neighbor's fenced yard, a rhizome barrier, or partial barrier, is the best method of control. A barrier system is reliable and trouble-free for most bamboos in most climates; however, bamboos with deep-running rhizome systems in soils that are loosely textured, warm, and moist to a depth of several feet (1 m or so) during the rhizome growth period could present containment concerns. Consult local bamboo growers with similar bamboos and growing conditions to more specifically assess control concerns and barrier requirements.

For this containment system, a barrier 2 to 3 ft. (60 to 90 cm) deep is inserted into the ground around the desired perimeter of the bamboo grove. Approximately 2 in. (5 cm) are left to protrude above ground to allow for a build-up of mulch from leaf fall or added materials and still provide a lip above the soil.

Once a year, in late fall or early spring, the barrier should be examined to ensure no rhizome has escaped over the top. In the rare event a rhizome leaps the barrier, it can be cut and pulled from the soil or simply repositioned inside the barrier. Ideally, the barrier should tilt outward slightly at the top so that any rhizomes colliding with the barrier will be directed upward.

Barriers may be made of a variety of materials. Concrete may work well in some situations, but it is heavy, bulky, and difficult to move or remove. Corrugated metal and fiberglass can deteriorate or break and are not recommended.

Increasingly, heavy plastic high density polyethylene (HDPE) is the material of choice. It is available from various bamboo nurseries and hardware stores, and can be cut to the length desired. It should be 60 mil thick and typically 2½ ft. (80 cm) wide. It is light, fairly attractive, easy to handle, and is not subject to cracking, corrosion, or decay. Thinner barrier material is sometimes sufficient, but may not be reliable over time, particularly with larger bamboos.

Bamboo is a superb, rapidly growing, evergreen privacy screen. This photo is taken from the homeowner's rooftop. From the living quarters, all windows of the adjacent home are screened. Barriers along the fence line control spread.

When positioning the plastic barrier, the seam should be without gaps and should overlap by a foot or two (30–60 cm). Ideally, the seam should be sealed with glue and rivets or small bolts, or some similar sealing and clamping method.

As an extra safety precaution, the seam should be situated where any compromise of the seal, and escape of a rhizome, would be readily apparent and manageable. For example, the seam should not be placed on the outer side of the clump or grove, adjacent to the fenced border of a neighbor's property, but on the inner side of the clump or grove, away from the fence.

The barrier area can be freely shaped to fit one's landscaping needs and preferences, but should not have any sharp turns that could abruptly turn a rhizome downward, or invite penetration by sharp-tipped rhizomes in the case of thinner barrier material.

A combination of a partial barrier and rhizome pruning can be an effective and preferred method in some applications. A barrier strip can be placed along a fence line with each end curved away from the fence. The open accessible portion is rhizome-pruned each year as described in the previous section, while the barrier portion prevents the bamboo from crossing the fence line. This combined method avoids a root bound condition in later years.

Shoot Removal

Shoot removal is a good method where precise control is not critical. Most bamboos shoot in spring and early summer. If a new shoot emerges where a culm is not wanted, simply remove the tender shoot by twisting or breaking it off at or slightly below soil level.

Shoot removal is not a good method when the incursion of rhizomes into other garden areas would be problematic, but in other situations, where some freedom is permitted, shoot removal is an excellent control method involving relatively little effort.

The harvest of shoots is a welcome boon for the table. Lawn mowing is a variant of the shoot removal method, though it does not offer a harvest of shoots as a benefit.

Containers

Most bamboos grow very well in containers, with the caveat that they will become root bound unless they are divided and repotted every couple of years. The container itself is the barrier for controlling spread. The drainage holes, however, are a potential source of escape for the rhizomes and should be checked once or twice a year. An escaping rhizome can simply be clipped off or tucked back into the container.

Bamboos are very light for their size, so one can have a portable landscape that can, for example, provide supplemental visual screening or shading for the patio in the summer or, in the winter, supplement screening that had been provided by a deciduous tree or shrub.

Controlling Height

If landscaping or other needs do not require bamboo within a specific height range, bamboo is best left unlimited. In landscaping and garden situations, however, it is often desirable to have bamboo grow within a specific height range. For example, a bamboo screen may need to grow sufficiently tall to block the view from a neighbor's window, but not so tall as to block the sun.

Various strategies can be employed to control height. Selecting bamboo according to its height potential is the most fundamental of these strategies.

In selecting bamboo for specific height ranges, one must consider growing conditions, size of the grove, and acceptable time for reaching the desired height. The maximum heights listed in this book represent what is possible for a large mature grove under ideal conditions. In most instances, a small grove in a typical landscaping situation will never attain the listed maximum height.

If a landscaping need calls for a screen at a height in the range of 15 to 20 ft. (4.6 to 6 m), for example, *Pseudosasa japonica*, a bamboo with a maximum height of about 18 ft. (5.5 m), would seldom be a good choice. In a small plot, even under ideal growing conditions, the plant would require many years to approximate the

New culms are growing much taller than the hedge height, but they can be topped at any time to maintain the desired height and preserve the distance view.

A bamboo hedge shields the home from the roadway. The bamboo is topped to the desired height so that the homeowner can enjoy both a distance view and privacy from the street.

desired height range, and even the minimum of the range might never be reached.

A much better choice might be *Phyllostachys bissetii*, *P. aureosulcata*, or even *P. nigra*, 'Henon' if growing conditions are particularly difficult. Although these species are capable of growing much taller than that desired for the screen, they can be maintained at a desired height, as we will discuss. It is much easier to limit the height of a taller bamboo than it is to stretch the growth potential of a smaller one.

Height can be controlled to some degree by modifying growing conditions or controlled more precisely by pruning to the desired height. Most bamboos with a height potential over 10 ft. (3 m) prefer sunny conditions and will grow less tall in partial shade.

The amount of water and fertilizer can be manipulated to control height. Particularly in drier growing areas, bamboo can be watered only enough to keep the grove healthy and within a desired height range. Minimal fertilizer will also limit growth, particularly in poor soils. These methods should be used only to limit vigor and not to the extent that the plant is unhealthy or wanting.

Pruning the top off a culm at the desired height is a very direct and precise way of limiting height. If much is removed, portions of the upper branches may need to be reduced to restore some of the culm's graceful taper. The cuts should always be made just above a culm or branch node to avoid unsightly ends.

Pruning and Thinning

Bamboo is easily one of the most beautiful landscape plants, yet lack of understanding often conspires against it, and the clumps or groves

In this bamboo garden, shrub and groundcover bamboo of various sizes and shapes lead the eye to the grove of the timber bamboo, *Phyllostachys edulis*, in the distance.

encountered in landscapes of the Western world are often tattered, unattractive thickets. A thoughtful thinning and pruning regimen will have a major impact on both the aesthetics and ongoing health of your bamboo.

Pruning is the removal of branches or parts of branches and culms. Topping to reduce height is a form of pruning. Pruning is not usually necessary for the health and vigor of a grove, but it can enhance aesthetics and broaden the use of bamboo in the landscape.

In addition to limiting height, top pruning is sometimes warranted to prevent wind or snow from breaking new culms or for keeping a bamboo with an arching habit more erect. Always make pruning cuts just above a culm or branch node so that branchless unsightly ends do not remain and deteriorate over time. Bypass pruning shears are ideal for lower branches; loppers

are handy for reaching higher; and pole loppers are necessary for reaching the tops of taller bamboos.

Bamboo is arguably the most beautiful when left to form its own natural shape, but pruning allows bamboo to be used in many more ways in the garden and landscape, and it allows specific bamboo to be used in ways that would otherwise be unsuitable.

For example, some bamboos, like *Phyllostachys bambusoides*, have a strongly upright habit, but others, like *P. nigra*, have an arching habit. With its black culms and branches, gracefully arching stature, and delicate foliage, *P. nigra* is among the most beautiful and graceful bamboos. Its arching habit, however, can be a problem in some settings if the arching culms block pathways or shade other plants. Topping the culms and pruning the upper branches reduces the arching tendency and may permit *P. nigra* to be planted where it might otherwise not be suitable.

Bamboo can also be pruned to form a beautiful hedge. Large-diameter bamboos, such as *Phyllostachys vivax*, will suffer and look odd if topped severely, but bamboo is generally amenable to major topping if required. It is quite feasible, for example, to maintain bamboo with a 50-ft.(15-m) height-potential topped and pruned to a 10-ft. (3-m) hedge. If a more severe hedge effect is desired, the side branches can be pruned in much the same manner as a conventional hedge, though the cuts should always be just above a node.

Just as a tree has more stature when its trunk is not covered to ground level by branches and foliage, so too, larger bamboos have more stature when the bases of their culms are not covered by foliage, but are exposed so that the masses of delicate foliage contrast and emphasize the stature and strength of the supporting culms. Removing the lowermost branches to expose the lower part of the culms can enhance bamboo's beauty.

Groundcover and small shrub-sized bamboos, particularly those with variegated leaves, can benefit from periodically trimming the outer foliage to renew its appealing freshness. Early spring is the best time to trim the plants, just before the new shoots, branches, and leaves emerge. Hedge trimming shears work well for many small bamboos. A large area of groundcover bamboo can be cut with a lawnmower.

Thinning is the removal of entire culms. It is essential for a healthy and attractive bamboo grove. The need for thinning applies to plantings of all sizes, from a bamboo forest covering many square miles to a small container on the patio. Only groundcover bamboo is not normally thinned, but it benefits from periodic pruning for some of the same reasons.

A shrubby *Chimonobambusa* emphasizing the foliage rather than the culms.

A healthy grove must be thinned so that sunlight can penetrate the foliage canopy. Damaged and misshapen culms are the first candidates for thinning. Next are the older culms and undersized culms.

Except for smaller bamboos grown as groundcovers or shrubs, most bamboos look best when spaced so that they appear as individual culms in the grove rather than as an indistinguishable part of a mass planting. This same aesthetic applies in a deciduous forest, as well as with other plants. Space makes the individual culms appear larger and gives stature to the culms as well as the grove. The contrast between sturdy culms and their delicate foliage is an essence of bamboo's beauty.

Although thinning can be done throughout the year, it is typically carried out midsummer through winter, after the shooting period is finished and well before the new season's growth begins. It is best to avoid thinning just before or during shooting, as the diminished energy reserves reduce the bamboo's ability to produce new shoots and culms.

Culms should never be thinned with a hatchet or an ax. This method damages the culm that is being harvested, risks damage to nearby culms and rhizomes, and leaves jagged stubs in the grove.

Bamboo culms should be sawed, flat across, at their base. The culms of subtropical and tropical bamboos are vulnerable to rot or rhizome damage and are usually sawed higher, always above a node, at roughly 4 to 8 in. (10 to 20 cm) or more above ground.

Large old clumps of bamboos with pachymorph rhizomes eventually become impacted at their centers if an ongoing thinning regimen is not followed. These clumps can be revitalized by cutting a path or section into the center of the clump, thus forming a horseshoe pattern with the remaining culms. This provides access to the center of the clump for additional thinning and management, and it clears away old growth, making way for healthy new growth in the clump's center.

Soil

Although bamboo is a tenacious survivor under adverse conditions and is not particularly fussy, the best soils promote rapid growth and the most attractive and productive groves. Bamboo prefers fertile soils rich in organic nutrients.

Ideal soils for most bamboos are slightly acidic, loosely textured, and well aerated. They should drain freely, yet retain moisture. Water-saturated, soggy, heavy soils exclude air from the root system, keep soil temperature low, and can cause rhizomes to rot.

Although the soil should be well cultivated and loose, it does not need to be cultivated very deeply. Even for large bamboos, cultivating to a depth of 2 ft. (60 cm) is generally sufficient.

Fertilizer

In general, a fertilizer mix suited to growing grass in a given area should also do well with bamboo. A fertilizer of phosphorus, potassium, and

Inside a thinned and well-maintained *Phyllostachys dulcis* grove.

a relatively higher amount of nitrogen is generally suitable. Bamboo responds very favorably to organic manures.

Fertilizer nutrients are most important to have available to the bamboo when the new shoots are forming underground. Depending on the local climate and type of fertilizer, late winter to midspring (February, March, or April in the Northern Hemisphere) is the prime time to begin the new year's fertilizing regimen for most bamboos. Timing will depend on the type of fertilizer and the amount of rainfall. Organic fertilizers may need to be applied earlier and helped by rain or watering to distribute the fertilizer to the root system. If liquid chemical fertilizers are used, their affects are more immediate.

In addition to being fertilized just prior to shooting, bamboo will benefit from lighter periodic applications spring through fall, and year-round for tropical and semitropical bamboos. Where winter freezing is a danger, caution must be exercised not to overfertilize in the fall or into winter. While it may be tempting to incorporate organic fertilizers in with winter's protective mulch, this could subject the bamboo to winter damage.

Water

Although most bamboos are relatively drought resistant, they only thrive with ample water. The roots, however, must not become waterlogged. Ideally, the soil should always be moist, but never soggy.

Ample soil moisture is one of the principal triggers that initiates shooting in many tropical and semitropical bamboos, because it signifies the beginning of the wet season and the period of active growth. For most bamboos, overwatering is not a concern as long as the soil is well aerated and free draining.

Bamboo also benefits from misting or vigorously spraying its foliage with water, particularly in drier climates. Misting or spraying creates a more locally humid environment, reduces plant stress, and discourages bamboo mites, aphids, and the like. Vigorously spraying the undersides of leaves will dislodge aphids and reduce or eliminate the black sooty mold that is their byproduct.

Mulch

Bamboo benefits greatly from a top mulch. A top mulch cycles nutrients back into the soil and tempers the effects of the environment by protecting bamboo from extremes of heat, cold, and drought. In areas with very severe winters, a winter layer of mulch 1 ft. (30 cm) or more deep may be essential for health and survival.

For most situations, a layer of mulch one to several inches (2 to 10 cm) deep will suffice. A mature grove provides its own mulch from leaf fall, but a new planting will benefit from augmentation.

Temperature and Light

USDA hardiness zones offer a rough guide to the relative hardiness of the various bamboos, but many factors are at play, including wind; humidity; soil moisture; snow cover; plant maturity; plant health; protection by structures, trees, and other plants; and duration and frequency of low temperatures. Zone ratings are only relative approximations of plant performance. A bamboo may tolerate a zone's minimum temperature for a night or two, but may not tolerate weeks at a temperature five degrees warmer.

Drying winds and the absence of snow cover might kill an immature plant outright, whereas a sheltered, more established plant might be entirely unscathed. The temperature zones in this book reflect exposure to minimum temperatures below which leaf damage may typically begin to occur.

In general, taller bamboos prefer full sun and shorter bamboos are typically understory plants that prefer some shade. Keep in mind, however, that the intensity of sunlight varies in different parts of the world. A bamboo that might prefer some shade in southern California or southern Europe might prefer full sun in the more northerly maritime influenced climates of the Pacific Northwest or England.

Other factors are at play as well. Many *Fargesia* bamboos need shade, but unlike most of the understory groundcover bamboos, *Fargesia* are intolerant of high temperatures. Many of the montane *Chusquea* bamboos thrive in full

A *Fargesia* bamboo provides color and textural contrast that underscores the impressive mass of the trees and graceful delicacy of the bamboo.

Asian garden themes are a natural for temperate climate bamboo.

Pests and Diseases

Various mammals pose a potential threat to bamboo. Bamboo shoots and foliage are attractive food sources for many animals, but circumstances vary, and the same mammal may present a major threat in one situation and no threat at all in another. For some mammals, such as mice, chipmunks, squirrels, and deer, eating bamboo is a learned response.

Voles and gophers can cause major damage at or below soil level, sometimes eating tender new shoots and rhizomes before they emerge from the ground.

Different control methods may be appropriate depending on circumstances. They include providing ready availability of a preferred food source, commercial repellents, shavings from aromatic deodorant soaps, hunting, trapping, poisoning, sound generators for the air or ground, fencing, wire or plastic screens for individual shoots, and underground mesh or surrounding gravel trenches for tunneling animals.

Bamboos in the tropics are under constant assault by a rich spectrum of insects, including various borers, defoliators, and sap suckers. Fortunately, for the North American and European gardener, the threat of bamboo pests and diseases is generally minimal, and usually confined to disfigurement or moderate damage.

Aphids are not a significant threat to the health of bamboo, but their excretions foster an unsightly, black, sooty mold. An infestation of mealybugs, a warm climate aphid relative, may appear as cottony deposits. Soap sprays, chemical sprays, or simply spraying with a strong jet of water will help keep aphid and mealybug populations in check.

Scales are another aphid relative that typically appear as bumps on the culms and branches of semitropical and tropical bamboos. They are unsightly, but generally do relatively little harm. Their exterior armor makes them resistant to insecticides except when immature. Scales can be picked off or scrubbed off with a plastic scouring pad.

A number of mite species are bamboo pests, but the bamboo mite is the major concern. Bam-

sun, but are intolerant of chronically warm soil temperatures and nighttime heat. *Phyllostachys* bamboos thrive in warm sunny conditions but most require a period of winter cold to maintain their vigor.

Many subtropical bamboos will grow in temperate climates if winter temperatures are not severe, but require warmer conditions for full size and vigor. These are not daunting prohibitions, but examples of considerations in choosing bamboo for one's growing conditions.

Most bamboos can grow successfully in a broad range of conditions, though the greatest vigor will occur in a narrower range. The great diversity among bamboo species ensures that a selection of bamboos can usually be found for most growing conditions. The A to Z listings in this book describe requirements and preferences in more detail.

Even a small grove can provide a tranquil sanctuary. Looking closely you can see the dark green chairs nestled in the grove. A narrow pathway leads to this peaceful retreat.

boo mites are difficult to eradicate. Colonies of these mites form a white protective web on the underside of foliage leaves. The mites feed by sucking fluid from the leaf cells, leaving large yellowed areas on the leaf to mark their progress. Mites thrive and rapidly multiply in high temperatures and low humidity.

Keeping bamboo well watered and periodically spraying or misting the foliage will help suppress mite infestation outbreaks. On a small scale, afflicted leaves can be removed by hand. Several miticides that are available in the nursery trade are effective. Total eradication may be possible if one has only a few, small plants, but if one has large plants, or a grove, suppression rather than total eradication may be the most feasible goal.

BAMBOOS FOR SPECIFIC PURPOSES AND LOCATIONS

The following lists may help you find bamboo selections to meet your gardening and landscaping requirements. The lists are not comprehensive and are far from exclusive. Many other bamboos, some less commonly available, may also work as well or even better for your particular needs. Treat these lists as a point of departure rather than a point of conclusion. Use them as a quick guide, then explore the A to Z section of this book to find the specific plants that are right for you and your garden.

Hardy Timber Bamboos
Phyllostachys bambusoides (most forms)
Phyllostachys edulis (all forms)
Phyllostachys makinoi
Phyllostachys nigra 'Bory'
Phyllostachys nigra 'Henon'
Phyllostachys nigra 'Megurochiku'
Phyllostachys viridis (all forms)
Phyllostachys vivax (all forms)

Hardy Medium-sized Bamboos
Chusquea gigantea
Phyllostachys angusta
Phyllostachys atrovaginata
Phyllostachys aurea (all forms)
Phyllostachys aureosulcata (all forms)
Phyllostachys bissetii
Phyllostachys heteroclada
Phyllostachys iridescens
Phyllostachys mannii
Phyllostachys nidularia
Phyllostachys nigra
Phyllostachys nuda
Phyllostachys platyglossa
Phyllostachys praecox (all forms)
Semiarundinaria fastuosa (all forms)
Semiarundinaria fortis

Hardy Small Bamboos
Borinda angustissima
Borinda fungosa
Chusquea culeou
Chusquea culeou 'Caña Prieta'
Chimonobambusa tumidissinoda
Fargesia murielae (all forms)
Fargesia nitida (all forms)
Fargesia robusta
Fargesia sp. 'Scabrida'
Hibanobambusa tranquillans 'Shiroshima'
Phyllostachys humilis
Pseudosasa japonica (all forms)
Semiarundinaria makinoi
Thamnocalamus crassinodus (all forms)

Hardy Shrub Bamboos
Indocalamus latifolius
Indocalamus tessellatus
Pleioblastus shibuyanus 'Tsuboi'
Sasa kurilensis 'Simofuri'
Sasa palmata
Sasa tsuboiana
Sasaella masamuneana (all forms)
Shibataea kumasaca
Yushania brevipaniculata

Hardy Groundcover Bamboos
Pleioblastus akebono
Pleioblastus distichus
Pleioblastus fortunei
Pleioblastus pygmaeus
Pleioblastus shibuyanus 'Tsuboi'
Pleioblastus viridistriatus (all forms)
Sasa veitchii
Sasaella masamuneana (all forms)
Sasaella ramosa

Opposite: Groundcover and shrub bamboos accent the landscape.

Hardy Clumping Bamboos

Borinda angustissima
Borinda contracta
Borinda fungosa
Borinda lushuiensis
Borinda papyrifera
Chusquea culeou
Chusquea culeou 'Caña Prieta'
Fargesia apicirubens
Fargesia denudata
Fargesia murielae (all forms)
Fargesia nitida (all forms)
Fargesia robusta
Thamnocalamus crassinodus (all forms)
Thamnocalamus tessellatus

Exceptionally Cold Hardy Bamboos

Arundinaria gigantea
Fargesia apicirubens
Fargesia dracocephala 'Rufa'
Fargesia murielae (all forms)
Fargesia nitida (all forms)
Fargesia robusta
Indocalamus tessellatus
Phyllostachys atrovaginata
Phyllostachys aureosulcata (all forms)
Phyllostachys bissetii
Phyllostachys mannii
Phyllostachys nuda
Phyllostachys rubromarginata
Phyllostachys vivax (all forms)
Pleioblastus distichus
Sasa nagimontana
Sasa palmata
Sasaella ramosa
Sasamorpha borealis
Semiarundinaria fastuosa (all forms)
Shibataea chinensis
Shibataea kumasaca
Yushania brevipaniculata

Bamboos for Shade

Fargesia murielae (all forms)
Fargesia nitida (all forms)
Himalayacalamus hookerianus
Pleioblastus akebono
Pleioblastus argenteostriatus

Pleioblastus fortunei
Pleioblastus viridistriatus (all forms)
Sasa kurilensis (all forms)
Sasa nagimontana
Sasa palmata
Sasa senanensis
Sasa tsuboiana
Sasa veitchii
Sasamorpha borealis

Variegated Bamboos

Bambusa multiplex 'Silverstripe'
Fargesia apicirubens 'White Dragon'
Hibanobambusa tranquillans 'Shiroshima'
Phyllostachys bambusoides 'Richard Haubrich'
Pleioblastus akebono
Pleioblastus argenteostriatus
Pleioblastus chino 'Kimmei'
Pleioblastus chino 'Murakamianus'
Pleioblastus chino 'Vaginatus Variegatus'
Pleioblastus fortunei
Pleioblastus shibuyanus 'Tsuboi'
Pleioblastus viridistriatus (all forms)
Sasa kurilensis 'Simofuri'
Sasaella masamuneana 'Albostriata'
Sinobambusa tootsik 'Albostriata'

Bamboos for Houseplants

Bambusa multiplex (all forms)
Bambusa ventricosa (all forms)
Bambusa vulgaris 'Vittata'
Chimonobambusa marmorea (all forms)
Chimonobambusa quadrangularis (all forms)
Chusquea cumingii
Chusquea delicatula
Chusquea pittieri
Chusquea tomentosa
Indocalamus tessellatus
Otatea acuminata (all forms)
Phyllostachys aurea (all forms)
Pleioblastus distichus
Pleioblastus fortunei
Pleioblastus pygmaeus
Pleioblastus viridistriatus (all forms)
Raddia distichophylla
Sasaella masamuneana (all forms)
Yushania anceps

Bamboos for Bonsai

Bambusa multiplex 'Riviereorum'
Bambusa multiplex 'Tiny Fern'
Bambusa ventricosa
Chimonobambusa marmorea (all forms)
Pleioblastus akebono
Pleioblastus chino 'Vaginatus Variegatus'
Pleioblastus distichus
Pleioblastus fortunei
Pleioblastus shibuyanus 'Tsuboi'
Pseudosasa owatarii

Bamboos for Borders and Low Hedges

Bambusa multiplex 'Riviereorum'
Pleioblastus chino (all forms)
Pleioblastus distichus
Pleioblastus fortunei
Pleioblastus pygmaeus
Pleioblastus shibuyanus 'Tsuboi'
Sasaella masamuneana 'Albostriata'
Shibataea kumasaca

Bamboos for Tall Hedges and Screens

Bambusa eutuldoides 'Viridivittata'
Bambusa malingensis
Bambusa multiplex (most forms)
Bambusa textilis (most forms)
Bambusa vulgaris 'Wamin'
Bambusa vulgaris 'Wamin Striata'
Borinda fungosa
Borinda lushuiensis
Borinda macclureana
Borinda papyrifera
Fargesia robusta
Fargesia sp. 'Scabrida'
Hibanobambusa tranquillans 'Shiroshima'
Himalayacalamus hookerianus
Phyllostachys angusta
Phyllostachys atrovaginata
Phyllostachys aurea (all forms)
Phyllostachys aureosulcata (all forms)
Phyllostachys bambusoides 'Allgold'
Phyllostachys bambusoides 'Castillon'
Phyllostachys bambusoides 'Kawadana'
Phyllostachys bissetii
Phyllostachys heteroclada
Phyllostachys humilis

Phyllostachys mannii
Phyllostachys nidularia
Phyllostachys nigra
Phyllostachys nuda
Pleioblastus simonii
Pseudosasa japonica
Semiarundinaria fastuosa (all forms)
Thamnocalamus tessellatus
Thyrsostachys oliveri
Thyrsostachys siamensis
Yushania anceps
Yushania boliana

Bamboos for Screens Two Stories or Higher

Bambusa lako
Bambusa oldhamii
Bambusa textilis (most forms)
Bambusa tuldoides
Bambusa vulgaris
Bambusa vulgaris 'Vittata'
Dendrocalamus asper
Dendrocalamus giganteus
Dendrocalamus latiflorus (all forms)
Phyllostachys aureosulcata (all forms)
Phyllostachys bambusoides (most forms)
Phyllostachys makinoi
Phyllostachys nigra 'Bory'
Phyllostachys nigra 'Henon'
Phyllostachys nigra 'Megurochiku'
Phyllostachys viridis (all forms)
Phyllostachys vivax (all forms)

Bamboos for Edible Shoots

Bambusa beecheyana
Bambusa membranacea
Bambusa oldhamii
Chimonobambusa quadrangularis
Chimonobambusa tumidissinoda
Dendrocalamus asper
Dendrocalamus brandisii
Dendrocalamus giganteus
Dendrocalamus hamiltonii
Phyllostachys atrovaginata
Phyllostachys aureosulcata (all forms)
Phyllostachys dulcis
Phyllostachys edulis (all forms)

Phyllostachys glauca
Phyllostachys iridescens
Phyllostachys nidularia (all forms)
Phyllostachys nuda
Phyllostachys platyglossa
Phyllostachys praecox (all forms)
Phyllostachys rubromarginata
Phyllostachys viridis (all forms)
Phyllostachys vivax (all forms)

Bamboos for Culm Wood
Bambusa membranacea
Bambusa textilis (all forms)
Dendrocalamus asper
Dendrocalamus giganteus
Gigantochloa atroviolacea
Guadua angustifolia
Phyllostachys angusta
Phyllostachys bambusoides (most forms)
Phyllostachys edulis
Phyllostachys makinoi
Phyllostachys meyeri
Phyllostachys nigra
Phyllostachys nigra 'Bory'
Phyllostachys nigra 'Henon'
Phyllostachys rubromarginata
Phyllostachys viridis (all forms)

Bamboos for Erosion Control
Arundinaria gigantea
Arundinaria tecta
Bashania fargesii
Chimonobambusa marmorea
Phyllostachys aurea (all forms)
Phyllostachys bissetii
Phyllostachys humilis
Pleioblastus chino (all forms)
Pleioblastus distichus
Pleioblastus pygmaeus
Sasa palmata
Sasaella masamuneana (all forms)
Sasaella ramosa
Semiarundinaria okuboi

Bamboos Tolerant of Alkaline Soils
Chusquea cumingii
Otatea acuminata subsp. *aztecorum*
Phyllostachys flexuosa (all forms)
Phyllostachys glauca
Phyllostachys mannii
Semiarundinaria fastuosa (all forms)
Yushania brevipaniculata

Bamboos Tolerant of Water-Saturated Soils
Chusquea culeou 'Caña Prieta'
Chusquea uliginosa
Phyllostachys atrovaginata
Phyllostachys heteroclada
Phyllostachys nidularia

Bamboos Tolerant of Salt Air
Chusquea culeou
Chusquea culeou 'Caña Prieta'
Pleioblastus gramineus
Pleioblastus hindsii
Pleioblastus linearis
Pleioblastus simonii (all forms)
Pseudosasa japonica (all forms)
Semiarundinaria fastuosa (all forms)
Semiarundinaria okuboi
Semiarundinaria yashadake (all forms)

Mite-Resistant Bamboos
Bashania fargesii
Borinda fungosa
Indocalamus latifolius
Indocalamus tessellatus
Phyllostachys dulcis
Phyllostachys edulis
Pleioblastus fortunei
Pleioblastus viridistriatus (all forms)
Semiarundinaria okuboi
Shibataea kumasaca

Timber Bamboos for Tropical and Semitropical Climates

Bambusa dolichoclada 'Stripe'
Bambusa lako
Bambusa membranacea
Bambusa oldhamii
Bambusa vulgaris (all forms)
Dendrocalamus asper
Dendrocalamus giganteus
Dendrocalamus latiflorus
Gigantochloa atroviolacea
Gigantochloa pseudoarundinacea
Guadua angustifolia
Thyrsostachys oliveri

Medium-sized Bamboos for Tropical and Semitropical Climates

Bambusa beecheyana
Bambusa multiplex (most forms)
Bambusa pachinensis
Bambusa textilis

Small Bamboos for Tropical and Semitropical Climates

Bambusa multiplex 'Fernleaf'
Bambusa multiplex 'Riviereorum'
Bambusa multiplex 'Fernleaf Stripestem'
Otatea acuminata subsp. *aztecorum*

Average Annual Minimum Temperatures for Plant Hardiness Zones

Temperature (°F)	Zone	Temperature (°C)
Below −50	1	Below −46
−50 to−40	2	−46 to −40
−40 to −30	3	−40 to −34
−30 to −20	4	−34 to −29
−20 to −10	5	−29 to −23
−10 to 0	6	−23 to −18
0 to 10	7	−18 to −12
10 to 20	8	−12 to −7
20 to 30	9	−7 to −1
30 to 40	10	−1 to 4
Above 40	11	Above 4

To see the U.S. Department of Agriculture Hardiness Zone Map, go to the U.S. National Arboretum site at http://www.usna.usda.gov/Hardzone/ushzmap.html.

BAMBOOS A–Z

ARUNDINARIA

In the 19th century, most Asian temperate and subalpine bamboos were heaped into the genus *Arundinaria*. Today, most of these bamboos have been moved to other genera. North America's only native bamboos belong to this genus.

Arundinaria comprises small to medium-sized shrublike or treelike bamboos with three to numerous principal branches, leptomorph rhizomes, and a running habit. Although usually smaller than those of *Phyllostachys*, the rhizomes of some *Arundinaria* species run more deeply and are more brittle, making management of lateral spread more difficult.

The leaves at the tip of a new shoot are closely arrayed in a fanlike cluster. The culm leaves are typically persistent and tend to convey a less pristine, more unkempt look in the landscape.

Arundinaria funghomii

Height: 4–30 ft. (1.2–9 m)
Diameter: 1 ⅛ in. (3 cm) max.
Light: mostly sunny
Zone 7
An attractive bamboo that may grow only 4 ft. (1.2 m) tall in cooler climates, *Arundinaria funghomii* shoots in late spring or summer. The new culms are densely covered with a gray bloom, handsomely setting off the dark green foliage.

Arundinaria gigantea
River cane, canebrake bamboo

Height: 10–33 ft. (3–9.9 m)
Diameter: 1 ½ in. (4 cm) max.
Light: full sun
Zones 5–6
A U.S. native bamboo that once covered thousands of acres and spanned a range from Mary-

Arundinaria funghomii, new culm showing gray bloom.

land, Virginia, and Florida, across to Texas, north to Missouri, and up the Ohio River Valley. The *Arundinaria gigantea* cane meadows provided food sources for herds of migrating buffalo, as well as for cattle and other domesticated animals. In some stands, the vegetation density was remarkable, reaching up to 65,000 culms per acre (160,000 culms per hectare). The canebrakes offered a unique habitat for nesting birds and other wildlife. The decimation or demise of Bachman's warbler, the passenger pigeon, and the Carolina parakeet has been attributed to the loss of the canebrakes.

Opposite: Contrasting sizes, shapes, and textures add interest to the garden. Here the foliage of *Semiarundinaria fastuosa* is set against the arborescent culms of the timber bamboo, *Phyllostachys vivax*.

Arundinaria gigantea

Arundinaria tecta

Although the species still extends over much of its former range, the acreage it covers is greatly diminished. Land clearing and overgrazing by livestock have decimated the once-great expanses of the native cane. Early settlers regarded canebrakes as indicators of fertile soil, and as a consequence, the canebrakes were subjected to intensive clearing for farmland.

Arundinaria gigantea exhibits considerable variation, culm coloration, and cold hardiness among the notable differences. Some variants are exceptionally cold hardy and show very little leaf withering, while other variants grown in the same conditions may be deciduous, regrowing leaves in the spring. *Arundinaria gigantea* can be reasonably attractive if well-maintained, though most would not regard it as a choice landscaping species. Most forms are cold hardy to zone 6.

'Macon'. A more upright, evergreen, cold-hardy variant from northern Tennessee and central Kentucky. Zone 5.

Arundinaria tecta
Switch cane
Height: 3–6 ft. (0.9–1.8 m)
Diameter: 1/2 in. (1.25 cm) max.
Light: full sun
Zone 6

Arundinaria tecta was once regarded as a subspecies of *A. gigantea*. The two have a close affiliation, but *A. tecta* is smaller with air canals in the rhizome system, more persistent culm leaves, and a scruffier and less desirable appearance. Different clones of *A. tecta* exhibit significant variation. Some variants are naturally deciduous in their native habitats, routinely dropping their leaves each winter.

BAMBUSA

A large genus comprising some 139 known species, *Bambusa* is endemic to the semitropical and tropical regions of the Old World. Some of its species, notably *B. vulgaris*, have been distributed and cultivated for so long throughout the tropics, including the New World, that it is often assumed that the genus is native to those areas as well.

Most members of the genus are large timber bamboos. All have pachymorph rhizome systems. Some species have a very tight clumping growth habit. Others have longer rhizome necks and form open clumps with more widely dispersed culms.

Bambusa species have a multiple branching habit with a principal branch that is generally significantly larger than the others. In a few species, thorny spines replace some of the branchlets. The culm leaf blades are erect and triangular. Culms are typically thick walled.

Several species of *Bambusa* have considerably greater cold tolerance than species of other semitropical and tropical genera. These can be successfully grown in temperate climates with mild winters, expanding the geographic reach of arborescent bamboo with a clumping habit—and giving the gardener, grower, and landscaper additional options. As the outer limits of cold tolerance are approached, however, the size and rate of growth is considerably reduced.

In most growing regions in the United States, shoot initiation naturally occurs in late summer to fall, presenting difficulties in marginal climates if the cold of winter arrives before the culms have finished shooting and hardening sufficiently, or before branching and leafing has been completed. As with other bamboo, if normal shooting and growth is disrupted, *Bambusa* will often initiate new shoots outside of its normal shooting interval.

Because *Bambusa* does not require a period of cold dormancy, the plants can successfully be grown indoors as houseplants if light and humidity are sufficient. The smaller ornamental species are particularly suited to this purpose.

Bambusa bambos
Giant thorny bamboo
Indian thorny bamboo
Height: 35–100 ft. (10.5–30 m)
Diameter: 7 in. (18 cm) max.
Light: full sun
Zone 10

Bambusa bambos is one of the most important bamboos in its native India. It is distributed throughout almost all of India and can be found at elevations up to nearly 4000 ft. (1200 m). In the Indian state of Maharashtra alone, *B. bambos* covers nearly 4900 square miles (12,750 sq.

Bambusa bambos

Bambusa beecheyana

km). This very vigorous tropical species is a tender bamboo, and is suited to only a few areas in North America. It grows well at the Quail Botanical Gardens in southern California, and thrives in southern Florida, generally shooting in the fall, but delaying branching until the following spring.

At the lower nodes, the branchlets are modified into sharp thorns, making an established clump nearly impenetrable by large animals. At the upper nodes, the branchlets become less thorny and more normally leaf bearing. The shoots are edible, but bitter, and require parboiling in at least two changes of water before they are ready for the table. Some sources regard them as excellent after parboiling. Because of its vigor and availability, *Bambusa bambos* has been used extensively in India for paper pulp production.

Bambusa beecheyana
Beechey bamboo
Height: 25–50 ft. (7.6–15 m)
Diameter: 5 in. (13 cm) max.
Light: full sun
Zone 9

Although fairly tolerant of cold, *Bambusa beecheyana* thrives and grows most vigorously in warm climates. New culms are covered by a white powder. The culms are elliptical in cross section and rapidly tapering. In southern China, it is a prime source of summer bamboo shoots.

The clump forms a fountain of arching culms. It is an attractive ornamental, but requires space, particularly in warm climates, where it grows large quickly. It was named for Captain F. W. Beechey, when a naturalist on his ship collected the species in Macao, in 1827.

Var. *pubescens*. Grows more erect and branches lower. Thickly hairy around the nodes.

Bambusa chungii
Height: 20–30 ft. (6–9 m)
Diameter: 2 in. (5 cm) max.
Light: full sun
Zone 9

The new culms are covered with a white waxy powder that gives them a beautiful soft blue coloration. *Bambusa chungii* is a highly desirable landscaping plant, though it has a somewhat open clumping habit and needs a bit more room than some of the tightest clumpers. *Bambusa chungii* comes from the lowland hills of southern China, where its thin-walled culms are used for weaving and handicrafts.

Var. *barbelatta*. A smaller variant that is about three-fourths the size.

Bambusa dolichoclada 'Stripe'
Height: 30–65 ft. (9–20 m)
Diameter: 4 in. (10 cm) max.
Light: full sun
Zone 9

Bambusa chungii

Bambusa dolichoclada 'Stripe'

Bambusa dolichomerithalla 'Silverstripe'

An attractive ornamental cultivated in Taiwan and southern Japan, *Bambusa dolichoclada* 'Stripe' has culms that are waxy yellow with dark green stripes.

Bambusa dolichomerithalla
Blowpipe bamboo
Height: 20–35 ft. (6–10.5 m)
Diameter: 2 in. (5 cm) max.
Light: full sun
Zone 9
Native to Taiwan and cultivated in Japan, *Bambusa dolichomerithalla* was introduced into the United States in 1980. Its common name, blowpipe bamboo, is derived from its long internodes and its traditional use as a blowpipe for cooking. It is found along streams and waterways at lower elevations.

'Green Stripestem'. Culms are yellow-green to orange-yellow, with dark green stripes on the internodes.

'Silverstripe'. Culms are dark green, with silver-white striping on the internodes.

Bambusa eutuldoides
Height: 20–45 ft. (6–14 m)
Diameter: 2¼ in. (6 cm) max.
Light: full sun
Zone 9
This species is widely cultivated in southern China, where the straight, thick-walled culms are used in constructing farm buildings and farm implements. Unusually, the culm leaf auricles differ greatly in size. One of the pair is five times as large as the other.

'Viridivittata'. Yellow culms with green stripes. Generally smaller than the primary form, and cultivated as an ornamental. Branches occur relatively low on the culm, making it a good choice for hedging or other screening.

Bambusa lako
Timor Black
Height: 25–50 ft. (7.6–15 m)
Diameter: 3½ in. (9 cm) max.
Light: full sun
Zone 10

Bambusa eutuldoides 'Viridivittata'

Bambusa lako

Bambusa lako is a choice ornamental bamboo. Its common name, Timor black, derives from its indigenous habitat on the island of Timor. The culms are initially green, turning brown-black to black with age, but retaining light green stripes. It is often mistaken for *Gigantochloa atroviolacea*, which it closely resembles. The culms of *B. lako* have a shiny surface, while those of *G. atroviolacea* have more of a matt finish. The shoots are edible.

Bambusa malingensis

Height: 20–35 ft. (6–10.5 m)
Diameter: 2½ in. (6.3 cm) max.
Light: full sun
Zone 9

A native of China's Hainan Island, *Bambusa malingensis* has strong culms that are used to make farm implements and frames for farmhouses. The lower branches may develop into soft or hard thorns. This bamboo forms tight erect clumps and is an excellent tall hedge plant. It is tolerant of strong winds and salty sea breezes.

Bambusa malingensis

Bambusa membranacea

Height: 30–70 ft. (9–21 m)
Diameter: 4 in. (10 cm) max.
Light: full sun
Zone 10

Until the late 1990s, *Bambusa membranacea* was classified as *Dendrocalamus membranaceus*. It is distributed in Burma, India, Laos, Thailand, and China. The culms are slender for their height and grow in loose clumps. The straight culms are used for construction and tools. The young shoots are choice for the table.

Bambusa multiplex
Hedge bamboo

Height: 3–30 ft. (0.9–9 m)
Diameter: 1½ in. (4 cm) max.
Light: full sun
Zone 9

One of the hardier of the semitropical bamboos, *Bambusa multiplex* is widely cultivated throughout the world as a windbreak and privacy hedge. It can be grown in the lower range of zone 9

Bambusa membranacea, new shoots in the fall.

Bambusa membranacea

Bambusa multiplex 'Alphonse Karr'

Bambusa multiplex 'Fernleaf'

climates and possibly in the upper ranges of zone 8 if conditions are otherwise favorable.

In China, the slender, thin-walled culms have been used in weaving and papermaking. The shoots are not amenable to the table, being quite bitter. This species does, however, excel as an attractive, clumping, hedge bamboo suited to a broad range of climate conditions, from the tropics to northern California and coastal climates even farther north.

The species has long been cultivated in many areas, and a number of distinctive ornamental cultivars have developed over time. The culms naturally arch, forming a rather broad hedge, but they take well to pruning and shaping, permitting a reasonably upright shape. Contributing to this bamboo's appeal as a hedge, culms form tight clumps and bushy branches grow low to the ground.

'Alphonse Karr'. Yellow culms with irregular green striping. The new culms often have a reddish blush, particularly when exposed to strong sunlight. A choice and widely cultivated ornamental.

'Fernleaf'. An unstable, smaller cultivar characterized by small, tightly spaced, closely two-ranked leaves. It generally retains its notable traits in infertile, drier conditions when its height is kept to no more than 10 ft. (3 m) or so. When offered better soil and moisture, 'Fernleaf' tends to grow taller and lose its fernlike features.

'Fernleaf Stripestem'. Similar to 'Fernleaf' but the culms are yellow with green stripes. The culms may turn reddish in the sun.

'Golden Goddess'. Similar to 'Fernleaf,' but the leaves are generally larger. The culms have a yellowish cast.

'Goldstripe'. Similar to the typical form, but the culms have a gold stripe that bleeds into the green.

'Midori Green'. Similar to the typical form, but the culms and branches are light green with darker green stripes.

'Riviereorum' (Chinese goddess bamboo). Grows to about 12 ft. (4 m) in warmer climates and only to about 6 ft. (1.8 m) in cooler climates.

Bambusa multiplex 'Fernleaf Stripestem'

It generally resembles 'Fernleaf', but is a stable form and maintains its low height and fernlike foliage. Its solid culms are a way to distinguish it from a small 'Fernleaf' plant. In the landscape, a slight breeze readily animates its lacy foliage. It is also an excellent houseplant, given sufficient light.

'Silverstripe'. The most vigorous cultivar of the species, 'Silverstripe' requires a warm climate and ample moisture to achieve its size potential. Like the other cultivars, it tolerates a wide range of conditions, from cool summers and winters to the conditions of a home interior. Many of the leaves are variegated with white

Bambusa multiplex 'Silverstripe'

Bambusa multiplex 'Riviereorum'

Bambusa nana (hort.)

striping. The culms also bear occasional thread-like white striping.

'Tiny Fern'. A dwarf form that typically only grows to a height of 3 ft. (90 cm). Its leaves are often less than 1 in. (2.5 cm) long. Small and delicate, 'Tiny Fern' is an excellent container plant.

'Tiny Fern Striped'. Similar to 'Tiny Fern' but with striped culms.

'Willowy'. The culms, branches, and twigs are exceptionally slender, and the leaves narrow. The culms have a very pronounced arching and drooping habit.

Bambusa nana (hort.)

Height: 12–20 ft. (4–6 m)
Diameter: 2 in. (5 cm) max.
Light: full sun
Zone 9

Bambusa nana is commercially cultivated in Thailand. In botanical literature, *B. nana* is an old synonym for *B. multiplex*; however, the *B. nana* of Thailand is a different species than *B. multiplex*. Although its botanical name may be in question, *B. nana* is nevertheless a very worthy bamboo. An appealing ornamental, it forms a tight clump with erect culms that are devoid of leaves on the lower nodes. The culms arch outward near the top to complete an attractive silhouette. The straight culms are also very strong and are highly desirable for construction when smaller-diameter culms are required.

Bambusa oldhamii
Giant timber bamboo
Oldham's bamboo

Height: 20–65 ft. (6–20 m)
Diameter: 4 in. (10 cm) max.
Light: full sun
Zone 9

Bambusa oldhamii is an attractive timber bamboo and the most commonly grown large tropical clumper in the United States. It thrives in southern California and Florida, where it reaches a height of 55 ft. (17 m). In warmer areas, such as Central America and China, it can grow even taller. Although the plant is relatively cold hardy, its maximum size is considerably smaller as warmth decreases. It has an erect habit, relatively short branches, and large, long leaves. Native to southern China, *Bambusa oldhamii* was introduced into Taiwan long ago, where it is now widely cultivated for its excellent tasting shoots.

For the smaller scale of many of today's landscaping needs, shorter more compact bamboos, such as *Bambusa textilis*, may be a better match, but when space permits, and where strong, dry winds are not a threat to its large leaves, the towering presence of *B. oldhamii* is impressive in the landscape. This bamboo takes well to pruning and makes a spectacular, tall hedge.

Bambusa oldhamii

Bambusa pachinensis

Height: 15–33 ft. (4.6–9.9 m)
Diameter: 2½ in. (6.3 cm) max.
Light: full sun
Zone 9

Indigenous to Taiwan and the mainland Chinese province of Fujian, *Bambusa pachinensis* was once classified as a variant of *B. textilis*. It is commonly employed as a windbreak in its native environment.

Bambusa textilis
Weaver's bamboo

Height: 15–50 ft. (4.6–15 m)
Diameter: 2 in. (5 cm) max.
Light: full sun
Zone 9

A choice landscaping bamboo native to China, *Bambusa textilis* has culms that grow strongly upright before nodding gracefully at their tips. The lower nodes are free of branches to a greater degree than most of the genus, up to as much as three quarters of the culm height in mature specimens, adding to its arborescent stature and ornamental appeal.

It has relatively small leaves for a semitropical bamboo and is better able to withstand strong, drying winds without damage to its foliage. The delicate foliage is attractive, matching the gracefulness of the rest of the plant.

It clumps very tightly, making an excellent hedge. Long internodes and strong but pliable fiber make it a choice bamboo for weaving all manner of materials, from delicate baskets to strong rope. The thin-walled, but strong, whole culms are used in craftwork and some furniture making.

Var. *albostriata*. White striping on the lower culm internodes and culm leaves. Native to China's Guangdong Province.

'Dwarf'. The smallest form of the species, but will still grow to 15–20 ft. (4.6–6 m).

Var. *glabra*. Slender, smooth, hairless culms and hairless sheaths.

Var. *gracilis*. Somewhat smaller with more slender culms. The foliage nods gracefully toward the top of the plant. A choice variant for the landscape.

Bambusa pachinensis

Bambusa textilis

Bambusa textilis forming an attractive backdrop.

'Kanapaha'. A larger variant of the species that can grow to 50 ft. (15 m). New culms have waxy powder and bluish cast.

'Maculata'. Smaller than the main form with subtle purple streaking on the culms and culm leaves.

'Mutabilis'. Long internodes with persistent bluish white waxy bloom on the internodes. Native to China's Hainan Island.

'Scranton'. Short branches give this variant a distinctive profile, particularly toward the top of the plant.

Bambusa tuldoides
Punting pole bamboo
Height: 30–55 ft. (9–17 m)
Diameter. 2 ¼ in. (6 cm) max.
Light: full sun
Zone 9

Native to China's Guangdong Province. Produces numerous culms, growing in a tight clump. The strong, thick-walled culm wood is used for construction. Traditionally the culms are used as punting poles to propel watercraft, hence its common name, punting pole bamboo. The shoots are edible.

Bambusa ventricosa
Buddha's belly bamboo
Height: 8–55 ft. (2.4–17 m)
Diameter: 2 ¼ in. (6 cm) max.
Light: full sun
Zone 9

A native of southern China. Highly dependent on environmental conditions for its appearance, it is most known for its form when potted, pruned, and stressed by withholding water. Under these conditions, the plant readily becomes dwarfed

Bambusa ventricosa showing moderate swelling of the internodes.

Bambusa tuldoides

and develops shortened, swollen internodes, hence its common name, Buddha's belly bamboo. When planted in the ground and given ample water and space, it exhibits a conventional habit, growing very tall without swollen internodes.

'**Kimmei**'. Yellow with a few green stripes. The culms can take on a pinkish cast.

Bambusa vulgaris

Height: 6–70 ft. (1.8–21 m)
Diameter: 5 in. (13 cm) max.
Light: full sun
Zone 10

An Old World bamboo, *Bambusa vulgaris* propagates easily and is one of the most widely distributed tropical bamboos in both the Old and New World. It was cultivated by Spanish colonists in southern Florida in the 1840s, and it may have been the first foreign species introduced into the United States. *Bambusa vulgaris* was also among the first bamboos introduced into Europe and was well established as a hothouse plant by the late 1700s.

Its rhizomes may extend up to 2½ ft. (80 cm) before turning upward, creating open, relatively fast-spreading clumps. *Bambusa vulgaris* is an attractive ornamental timber bamboo. The culm wood is starchy and relatively soft, but the culms are often used for scaffolding and basic construction. Its shoots are edible, though bitter. This species has never had a period of gregarious flowering that periodically decimates most other bamboos.

'**Vittata**'. Golden-yellow culms with green vertical striping of varying widths. New culm leaf sheaths are green with yellow striping. A highly attractive, large ornamental bamboo.

Bambusa ventricosa 'Kimmei' showing less-pronounced swelling of the internodes.

Bambusa vulgaris

Bambusa vulgaris 'Vittata'

'Wamin'. When stressed, this variant has swollen, highly shortened internodes on the lower portion of the plant, dwarfing it to 6–16 ft. (1.8–5 m). An unusual looking ornamental that some find appealing. The exaggerated features, however, are dependent upon growing conditions. Unstressed plants often look more conventional.

'Wamin Striata'. Similar to 'Wamin' with contrasting light and dark green stripes.

BASHANIA

Rugged and hardy, *Bashania* species are endemic to the mountainous regions of central China, where they share forest habitats with broad-leaved trees and conifers. They are also sometimes found in pure stands. These medium sized bamboos have leptomorph rhizomes and a vigorously running habit.

Bashania fargesii
Windbreak bamboo
Height: 15–25 ft. (4.6–7.6 m)
Diameter: 2 in. (5 cm) max.
Light: mostly sunny
Zone 7

Bambusa vulgaris 'Wamin Striata' showing a modestly developed swollen internode on an unstressed plant.

Bashania fargesii

Distributed in the Shaanxi, Hubei, and Gansu Provinces of China, *Bashania fargesii* has thick culm walls and an erect habit. The tough, robust leaves are broader and longer than those of *Phyllostachys* bamboos. Initially, there are three branches at each node, later becoming many. An aggressive runner, the plant withstands strong winds and makes an excellent windbreak. The culm and branch leaf sheaths are persistent or late in shedding giving the bamboo a somewhat less kempt look than *Phyllostachys* bamboos.

BORINDA

Borinda species are highly attractive, Old World, montane bamboos with pachymorph rhizomes and a clumping habit. Many of them are cold hardy, though less so than the most cold-hardy species of *Fargesia*.

The leaves are typically thin, soft, and pliable, with a matt finish. High-altitude species are deciduous in the winter. New shoots often have a tuft of long, generally erect, leaf blades at the apex. New culms of many species have a bluish white waxy bloom.

In their native habitats, borindas are distributed along a continuous chain of mountain ranges, from Annapurna in western Nepal and Tibet, across to China's Yunnan Province, and down to within 150 mi. (240 km) of Ho Chi Minh City (Saigon) in southern Vietnam. They are found at elevations ranging from 6000 to 13,800 ft. (1800 to 4200 m).

Like most montane bamboos, borindas are not well suited to high heat and humidity. They are generally not recommended for warm climates such as those of most of the U.S. Southeast.

Borinda albocerea
Height: 12–20 ft. (4–6 m)
Diameter: 1 in. (2.5 cm) max.
Light: partial shade
Zone 8
The species name means white wax, and the white waxy powder on the new culms produces a prominent bluish coloration. Mature culms turn

Borinda albocerea

creamy yellow. The culm leaves persist for a time before dropping away. A desirable ornamental introduced to the Western world in the 1990s from Yunnan, China.

Borinda angustissima
Height: 12–20 ft. (4–6 m)
Diameter: ³⁄₄ in. (2 cm) max.
Light: partial shade
Zone 8
Native to the evergreen, broad-leaved forests of Sichuan, *Borinda angustissima* is used for weaving and provides food for the giant panda. New shoots are purple to purple-green. Young culms

Borinda angustissima

Borinda contracta

Borinda fungosa

are heavily covered with white powder. This bamboo forms a very tight clump, and the slender culms and small narrow leaves give the plant a delicate elegance.

Borinda contracta
Height: 10–16 ft. (3–5 m)
Diameter: 3/4 in. (2 cm) max.
Light: partial shade
Zone 8
Native to Yunnan, China, at elevation ranges of 6600 to 10,000 ft. (2000 to 3000 m). The nearly solid culms are a waxy bluish-gray when young, turning to grayish green with age.

Borinda fungosa
Height: 12–20 ft. (4–6 m)
Diameter: 1 in. (2.5 cm) max.
Light: partial shade
Zone 8
Native to China's Yunnan and Sichuan Provinces at an elevation range of 6000 to 8900 ft. (1800 to 2700 m). The leaves are large and lush for a montane bamboo, up to 6 1/4 in. (16 cm) long and 2/3 in. (1.7 cm) wide.

A choice ornamental, the culms turn a beautiful deep brownish red when exposed to sun. The leaves often to bleach out after a hard winter, but in the spring as the color migrates back from

Borinda lushuiensis

yellowish green to lime green, the leaf coloration is distinctive and strikingly beautiful against the dark culms and branches.

Young plants are notably cold sensitive and may be deciduous in marginal conditions, but this species is among the more heat tolerant montane bamboos. Though small, the shoots are good tasting without bitterness.

'White Cloud' Leaves with some white striping. Slightly smaller and less cold hardy.

Borinda lushuiensis
Height: 16–40 ft. (5–12 m)
Diameter: 2 in. (5 cm) max.
Light: partial shade
Zone 8

Among the largest and most vigorously growing of the Old World montane bamboos. The range of coloration is quite spectacular—red, pink, and green culm sheaths, and waxy blue new culms changing to various shades of lime green, gray-green, and olive.

From Yunnan, China, at an elevation of 6000 ft. (1800 m). It is among the less cold hardy of the species, and may be marginal in zone 8. Its size, vigor, and beauty set it apart from all but a few Old World montane bamboos.

Borinda macclureana
Height: 14–30 ft. (4.3–9 m)
Diameter: 1¾ in. (4.4 cm) max.
Light: partial shade
Zone 7

Native to spruce, pine, and oak forests of southeastern Tibet, at an elevation range of 6900 to 12,500 ft. (2100 to 3800 m), where it is the dominant understory plant. Its native habitat is relatively dry. It will likely prove to

Borinda lushuiensis, multifaceted coloration in new shoots and culms

Borinda macclureana

Borinda macclureana. In a developing clump, new culms rise above the previous year's growth.

be among the more robust and hardier of the genus. With leaves that are relatively large for a Himalayan montane bamboo and its tall stature and sturdy culms, it is an impressive specimen plant.

Borinda nujiangensis

Height: 12–20 ft. (4–6 m)
Diameter: 1³⁄₈ in. (3.5 cm) max.
Light: partial shade
Zone 8
From Yunnan, China at an elevation range of 8200 to 9500 ft. (2500 to 2900 m). Long narrow leaves are among the smallest of the genus. The culm walls are thick. Sheaths on new culms are mottled red.

Borinda papyrifera

Height: 14–30 ft. (4.3–9 m)
Diameter: 2 in. (5 cm) max.
Light: partial shade
Zone 8
From western Yunnan, China, near the Burmese border, at an elevation of 8900 to 11,800 ft. (2700 to 3600 m). The culm sheaths have pastel color tones. The new culms are a luminescent powdery blue-white, changing to deep yellow with age.

Borinda papyrifera has a sturdy appearance, with a relatively upright growth habit. The culms are spaced somewhat widely apart. The shoots are edible. The nearly solid, finely striated culms are used for weaving and tools.

Borinda nujiangensis

Borinda papyrifera

Borinda perlonga

Borinda sp. 'Muliensis'

Borinda perlonga
Height: 12–20 ft. (4–6 m)
Diameter: 1½ in. (4 cm) max.
Light: partial shade
Zone 8
Less waxy powdery coating on new culms than some of the species. Older culms have a pronounced arch, sometimes drooping to the ground. Culm leaves are persistent and much longer than the internodes. Very late shooting that may not begin until fall.

Borinda sp. 'KR 5288'
Height: ?
Diameter: ?
Light: partial shade
Zone 8
A recent introduction. New unbranched culms grow tall and erect, then droop to the ground

as foliage emerges, creating a mounded effect. Unusual and attractive, but not for small spaces.

Borinda sp. 'Muliensis'
Height: 4–6 ft. (1.2–1.8 m)
Diameter: ⅓ in. (0.8 cm) max.
Light: partial shade
Zone 8
From Sichuan, China. Species not yet determined. The broad leaves have a deciduous propensity in winter.

Borinda yulongshanensis
Height: 12–22 ft. (4–6.6 m)
Diameter: 1 in. (2.5 cm) max.
Light: partial shade
Zone 6
From northwestern Yunnan, China at an elevation of 9800 to 13,800 ft. (2940 to 4200 m).

Borinda sp. 'KR 5288'

Borinda yulongshanensis

Cephalostachyum pergracile

Cold hardiness undetermined, but may be the hardiest of the genus since it thrives at such high elevations in its native environment.

New culms are bluish green, turning purplish with age. The sheaths are vibrant purple and unusually hairy. The culm sheaths cling with some persistence.

CEPHALOSTACHYUM

Cephalostachyum includes tropical bamboos with pachymorph rhizome systems that range in appearance from shrublike to climbing to tall and treelike. The culms are generally slender and thin walled. The genus consists of some 16 known species.

Cephalostachyum pergracile
Height: 20–40 ft. (6–12 m)
Diameter: 2¾ in. (7 cm) max.
Light: full sun
Zone 10
A tender, tropical bamboo known for both its beauty and utility. Native to India, Burma, and Thailand, and widely cultivated in China's Yunnan Province, it is a very attractive arborescent bamboo with tufted foliage and nodding culm tips. The culm leaf sheaths are shiny, leathery, and chestnut brown, covering about a third of the internode. It is a striking specimen in the landscape. Locally, rice is boiled in the culm joints, flavoring the rice and making a convenient carrying vessel for travel.

CHIMONOBAMBUSA

Comprising some 37 species, *Chimonobambusa* bamboos typically spread aggressively and range in size from shrublike to medium-sized and semi-arborescent. Unusual for bamboos with leptomorph rhizomes, some species shoot in the fall rather than spring.

Although well adapted to its native environments, chimonobambusas do not always fit perfectly in other climates. Some species are moderately winter hardy, but the tender shoots that come in fall and winter are readily susceptible to cold damage, disrupting the plant's growing cycle. If fall and winter shoots are damaged or

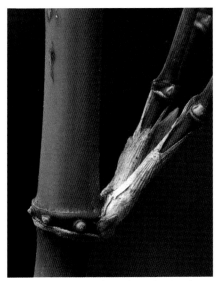

Chimonobambusa quadrangularis, showing the aerial roots or spines on the nodes characteristic of some species in the genus.

destroyed, these bamboos often compensate by shooting again in the spring and summer.

In China, *Chimonobambusa* species are found at elevations of 300 to 8500 ft. (90 to 2600 m) in high humidity environments. The lower-elevation species tend to shoot in the fall, the higher-elevation species in the spring. They are understory plants that thrive when the forest canopy reduces sunlight by about 60 percent.

Typically there are three primary branches at each node. Culms are squarish in some species. The nodes are often distinctive, broad and exceptionally exaggerated in some species, or with root thorns on the lower nodes in other species.

Chimonobambusa macrophylla 'Intermedia'

Height: 3–10 ft. (0.9–3 m)
Diameter: 1/2 in. (1.25 cm) max.
Light: partial shade
Zone 7
Native to Sichuan, China. Somewhat swollen nodes, but not as distinctively exaggerated as *Chimonobambusa tumidissinoda*. A shrubby bamboo with somewhat larger leaves than most

Chimonobambusa macrophylla 'Intermedia'

others of the species. It is reasonably attractive, but rather nondescript.

Chimonobambusa marmorea
Marbled bamboo

Height: 3–8 ft. (0.9–2.4 m)
Diameter: 1/2 in. (1.25 cm) max.
Light: partial shade
Zone 8
Its name, marbled bamboo, derives from the marbled purple and cream coloration of the new shoots and culm leaf sheaths. New shoots are initially without branches, branching out near the top of the culm the following summer, then branching further down the culm in subsequent years. Culm leaves are longer than the internodes and tardy to shed. The culms turn a vivid

Chimonobambusa marmorea

red with sun exposure. An aggressive runner, it can be very attractive, but requires more maintenance to look its best.

'Variegata'. Foliage leaves have narrow white stripes.

Chimonobambusa quadrangularis
Square bamboo

Height: 10–25 ft. (3–7.6 m)
Diameter: 1½ in. (4 cm) max.
Light: mostly sunny
Zone 8

Native to southeastern China. An attractive ornamental bamboo with distinctive squarish culms, a feature most pronounced in established groves with mature culms. The lower nodes have small, spinelike root thorns. The culm walls are thick, but not very strong. They are used as walking sticks and for craft items, but are unsuitable for construction or weaving.

The shoots, coming in the fall, are regarded as choice edibles, but the tender new culms are at risk of winter damage in marginal climates. Replacement shoots may grow in spring or summer, but the plant may be substantially smaller than its maximum size potential.

Chimonobambusa marmorea
'Variegata'

Chimonobambusa quadrangularis
'Suow'

Chimonobambusa quadrangularis
'Yellow Groove'

'Joseph de Jussieu'. Yellow culms with a green sulcus and some green striping. Leaves have some white striping.

'Suow'. Soft yellow culms with green stripes of varying widths.

'Yellow Groove'. Green culms with a yellow sulcus.

Chimonobambusa tumidissinoda
Chinese walking stick bamboo
Height: 10–20 ft. (3–6 m)
Diameter: 1¼ in. (3.2 cm) max.
Light: partial shade
Zone 7

Unique and attractive and the subject of Chinese myth and legend, the species name is derived from its tumid, or exceptionally swollen, nodes. The nodes are said to have the shape of two dinner plates placed face to face. It is also commonly known by its former botanical name, *Qiongzhuea tumidissinoda*. The distinctive culms are used as walking sticks. Shoots, coming in the spring, are exceptionally choice edibles, both fresh and dried.

One of the higher elevation of the genus, its native habitat are hilltops in northeastern Yunnan and southwestern Sichuan, at an altitude range of 5000 to 7200 ft. (1500 to 2200 m). It flourishes in an environment of abundant rainfall, moderate sun, high humidity, and acid soil, forming dense thickets in its native environment.

It is a beautiful but highly aggressive runner. Excess sun causes the delicate sprays of foliage to turn yellowish green. Shade fosters a rich, deep green.

CHIMONOCALAMUS
A genus of clumping bamboos with pachymorph rhizomes, *Chimonocalamus* is comprised of species native to the mountainous subtropical regions in Yunnan, China; Tibet; northeastern India; Bhutan; and Burma. There are some 16 known species, but cultivation in the West is rare.

Chimonocalamus are shrubby to moderately arborescent bamboos with three to five branches

Chimonobambusa tumidissinoda

Chimonobambusa tumidissinoda, showing the smooth, exceptionally swollen node.

Chimonocalamus pallens

per node. The culm leaves are usually longer than the internodes and are readily deciduous. Lower nodes typically have thorny root primordia. New shoots generally appear in spring to midsummer.

The genus is notable for its excellent-tasting bamboo shoots and is known in China as *xiang zhu*, "fragrant bamboo." The culms are used for implements and construction.

Chimonocalamus pallens
Gray bamboo

Height: 12–26 ft. (4–7.8 m)
Diameter: 2 in. (5 cm) max.
Light: mostly sunny
Zone 8

From the broadleaved evergreen forests in southern Yunnan, China, at elevations of 4600 to 6600 ft. (1400 to 2000 m). The name pallens, or pale, references the gray-green coloration of the new culms. In China it is known as gray bamboo and is cultivated as an ornamental. New shoots come in early to midsummer.

CHUSQUEA

A New World counterpart to the Old World's mountain bamboos, *Chusquea* is associated with the Andes, just as many of the Old World's mountain bamboos are associated with the Himalayas. The natural habitat for *Chusquea* ranges from northwestern Mexico to the West Indies to southern Chile and Argentina, at altitudes ranging from sea level to more than 14,000 ft. (4300 m), from tropical lowlands to high-altitude grasslands and pine forests.

Many chusqueas inhabit open, high-elevation grasslands that are windy, humid, and rainy. Daily temperature fluctuations typically exceed seasonal fluctuations. The nights are cool, dipping to near freezing or below, followed by daytime temperatures sometimes reaching to the upper 60s (about 20°C).

Although most chusqueas inhabit higher elevations and montane environments, where precipitation is primarily received in the form of fog and mist, some species are native to the hot, sunny lowlands. More than a third of the named *Chusquea* species and the majority of the undescribed species are indigenous to the Andes.

From both a latitude and altitude standpoint, *Chusquea* has a broader distribution than any other bamboo genus. Of an estimated 200 *Chusquea* species, only about two thirds have yet been named and taxonomically described.

Bamboo culms are usually hollow, but most *Chusquea* species have solid culms. Most chusqueas also have pachymorph rhizomes and form clumps that range from tightly grouped to open and moderately spreading. While nearly all bamboos form multiple branches from a single bud per node, most chusqueas have many buds per node, some more dominant than others, in patterns that are distinctive to the species.

Although a few chusqueas are quite cold hardy, most are relatively tender, which would seem to limit them to the warmest parts of the United States and Europe. Yet, many of the hardier chusqueas are not heat tolerant either. Warm nights and warm soil temperatures are particularly problematic for many of the species.

A few species do match up quite well with some North American and European growing climates. In particular, the U.S. West Coast and the United Kingdom offer suitable growing conditions for a number of chusqueas. Many of the chusqueas are listed as zone 9, but may be marginal in the colder reaches of that zone, particularly if other conditions are less than ideal.

Chusqueas are unusual and appealing bamboos, and it is worth the effort to explore them if one's climate permits.

Chusquea andina
Height: 4–12 ft. (1.2–4 m)
Diameter: 1 in. (2.5 cm) max.
Light: mostly sunny
Zone 7

Closely related to *Chusquea culeou*, this species is perhaps the most cold hardy of the genus, growing above the tree line in its native habitats of central Chile and Argentina. The small, stiff, spiky leaves are a uniquely striking blue color.

Chusquea circinata
Height: 12–22 ft. (4–6.6 m)
Diameter: 1 in. (2.5 cm) max.
Light: mostly sunny
Zone 9
From central and southern Mexico. Dark arching culms. *Chusquea circinata* somewhat resembles *C. coronalis*, but is not quite as ornamentally impressive. The subsidiary branches of *C. circinata* are coarser and more erect, and the foliage leaves are narrower. The branches grow in a

Chusquea andina

Chusquea circinata, complex branching pattern on a new culm.

Chusquea circinata

Chusquea coronalis

whorl around the circumference of the culm, and spinelike root thorns form at the nodes. Newly emerging branches on black culms are striking.

'Chiapas'. From a lower altitude. The leaves are slightly larger. Slightly less cold hardy.

Chusquea coronalis

Height: 12–23 ft. (4–7 m)
Diameter: ¾ in. (2 cm) max.
Light: partial shade
Zone 9

A highly desirable but somewhat temperamental ornamental, *Chusquea coronalis* is native to warm lowlands and cloud forests from Mexico to Costa Rica. The branches grow in a whorl around the circumference of the culm. Delicate, with a profusion of subsidiary branches and foliage leaves arrayed more or less horizontally.

One of the more widely cultivated bamboos of the genus, it prefers a moist habitat and moderate sun. In cultivation in North American and European climates, it typically experiences a significant leaf drop in winter, leafing out again and regaining its delicate attraction with the changing seasons. Dry, indoor conditions, particularly in winter, will cause it to suffer. May require full shade in Zone 10 climates.

Chusquea culeou

Height: 12–25 ft. (4–7.6 m)
Diameter: 1½ in. (4 cm) max.
Light: mostly sunny
Zone 7

A dominant understory plant in the southern Andean beech forests of its native Argentina and Chile, forming dense stands where the overstory has been disturbed or eliminated, such as by fire or logging. Among the most widely cultivated of all the chusqueas, finding its way to both American and European gardens, *Chusquea culeou* is one of the hardiest of the genus.

It is among the few chusqueas in which there is no pronounced difference in branching size between the central branch bud and the subsidiary buds, the multiple branches all appearing generally equal.

Chusquea culeou is quite varied in form, perhaps indicating a progression to formation of new species. Leaf size of some forms is up to three times larger than that of other forms. It also responds to environmental conditions by varying its form. Under strong sun, *C. culeou* has a more compact, shrubby form, with smaller branches. In more shaded conditions, it is taller with longer branches and a more open habit. Culms are erect to leaning. Individual culms may live up to 33 years.

Chusquea culeou

Chusquea culeou 'Hillier'

Chusquea culeou 'Caña Prieta'

'Argentina'. Longer, less compact branches. At one time regarded as a separate species.

'Caña Prieta'. Smaller and more delicate than the standard form. The cultivar name 'Caña Prieta' is derived from the Spanish words meaning blackish or very dark cane. The culms turn a very dark red-brown that is sometimes almost black. The culm leaves may persist, looking slightly disheveled, but they eventually disintegrate and diminish. Prefers acidic soil to thrive and look its best, but will do well in soils that are only moderately acidic.

'Hillier'. Smaller, compact, with short branches.

Chusquea cumingii
Height: 4–12 ft. (1.2–4 m)
Diameter: ¾ in. (2 cm) max.
Light: full sun
Zone 7
Native to semiarid regions of central Chile, *Chusquea cumingii* has distinctive, small, stiff, sharply pointed, prickly leaves, with a blue-green colorcast and matt finish. The leaf characteristics are most prominent when grown in full sun. Prefers somewhat alkaline soil, though also does well in slightly acidic soil.

Chusquea culeou 'Argentina'

Chusquea cumingii

Chusquea cumingii, branches and stiff prickly leaves.

Chusquea delicatula, tufted leaves and branches.

Chusquea foliosa, branching pattern.

Chusquea delicatula

Sometimes clambering, it can also form large impenetrable mounds. As a small plant, or when growth is controlled to desired limits, it is distinctive and attractive.

Chusquea delicatula

Height: 8–12 ft. (2.4–4 m)
Diameter: ¼ in. (0.6 cm) max.
Light: mostly sunny
Zone 10
Native to Peru and Bolivia. Thin culms with a clambering habit. Beautiful delicate leaf tufts and branches.

Chusquea foliosa

Height: 15–65 ft. (4.6–20 m)
Diameter: 2 in. (5 cm) max.
Light: mostly sunny
Zone 9
Indigenous to Chiapas, Mexico, and the montane, oak, cloud forests of Costa Rica, at elevations of 7200 to 8500 ft. (2200 to 2600 m). Common on the slopes of Costa Rican volcanoes. Culms erect at base, then arching. Long, drooping, narrow leaves. A very desirable ornamental.

Chusquea foliosa

Chusquea gigantea

Chusquea gigantea, branch buds showing unequal size.

Chusquea gigantea

Height: 16–60 ft. (5–18 m)
Diameter: 2¼ in. (6 cm) max.
Light: full sun
Zone 7

Formerly in the garden trade under the name *Chusquea breviglumis*; however, some of these plants are simply *C. culeou*. *Chusquea gigantea* is closely related, but can readily be distinguished by its one to three branch buds that are much larger than the other subsidiary buds, rather than the uniform array typical of *C. culeou*.

In an individual culm's second year, an additional one to three new large buds appear and generate even larger primary branches. In my relatively small clump, a central branch on one 14 ft. (4.3 m) tall culm measured nearly 5 ft. (1.5 m) in length.

As with most chusqueas, *Chusquea gigantea* performs far better in the ground than in a container. It is an exceptionally vigorous plant, and its pachymorph rhizomes have rather long necks, creating an open, relatively rapidly spreading clump. The culms quickly increase in size from year to year.

The partially red-brown culms can be striking, though they are often partially covered with tattered culm leaves, giving a slightly unkempt appearance. Stripping the culm leaves enhances the plant's appearance, as does pruning back the large dominant branches if they get out of hand. Not the most elegant of bamboos, but striking in its own way.

Chusquea glauca

Height: 8–20 ft. (2.4–6 m)
Diameter: ½ in. (1.25 cm) max.
Light: mostly sunny
Zone 9

From the cloud forests of eastern central Mexico at an elevation range of 4300 to 7200 ft. (1300 to 2200 m). Large tropical-looking leaves, probably the largest of the genus. Unusually for bamboo, the undersides of the leaves have a waxy coating. Vining and clambering in its native habitat, though it can stand on its own without support.

Chusquea glauca

Chusquea liebmannii

Chusquea mimosa
subsp. *australis*

Chusquea liebmannii

Height: 15–33 ft. (4.6–9.9 m)
Diameter: 1 in. (2.5 cm) max.
Light: mostly sunny
Zone 10
Native to dry habitats of pine and oak forests
from Mexico to Costa Rica and can tolerate periods of total dryness. Ironically, one of the few of
the genus that thrives in the heat and humidity
of southern Florida.

Arching, clambering habit. Spinelike roots at
the nodes. Branches grow in a whorl around
the circumference of the culm. Unlike most
bamboos, when stressed, the leaf blades fold
together along their length rather than rolling
up. Shorter and bushier in full sun. Can be used
as arbor or house plant.

Chusquea mimosa subsp. *australis*

Height: 8–16 ft. (2.4–5 m)
Diameter: 1 in. (2.5 cm) max.
Light: partial shade
Zone 9
Native to cloud forests, canyons, stream banks,
and marshy areas of southeastern Brazil. A highly

Chusquea mimosa subsp. *australis*, branching
pattern.

attractive ornamental with dark culm leaves and
branches with whorls of small leaves. An uncommon feature for chusqueas, the culm leaves drop
away to expose the new branches.

Chusquea pittieri

Chusquea pittieri, thorny root primordia on lower nodes.

Chusquea sp. 'Chiconquiaco', spiderlike appearance of new branches.

Chusquea sp. 'Las Vigas'

Chusquea subtilis

Chusquea pittieri

Height: 20–65 ft. (6–20 m)
Diameter: 2 in. (5 cm) max.
Light: full sun
Zone 9

One of the largest and most robust of the chusqueas. Native to Central America and Mexico where it forms dense stands on canyon walls, covering them with cascading foliage, or threads its way into trees, arching or hanging on convenient supports. Attractive on a smaller scale as a house plant. Thorny root primordia are prominent on the lower nodes.

Chusquea sp. 'Chiconquiaco'

Height: 8–15 ft. (2.4–4.6 m)
Diameter: ¹/₂ in. (1.25 cm) max.
Light: mostly sunny
Zone 9

Collected from a cloud forest in Veracruz, Mexico. Small leaves and thin culms. Spreading habit, clambering into trees or cascading down slopes.

The culm leaves have a friction stickiness resembling that of a cat's tongue.

Chusquea sp. 'Las Vigas'

Height: 6–12 ft. (1.8–4 m)
Diameter: ¹/₂ in. (1.25 cm) max.
Light: mostly sunny
Zone 9

Moderately large leaves. Arching culms and a clambering habit. New shoots are vivid pinkish red.

Chusquea subtilis

Height: 12–20 ft. (4–6 m)
Diameter: 1 in. (2.5 cm) max.
Light: mostly sunny
Zone 9

Indigenous to the Talamanca Range of Costa Rica at elevations of 8370 to 9800 ft. (2550 to 3000 m). Numerous branches per node and long, narrow foliage leaf blades. Resembles *Chusquea foliosa* but reportedly easier to grow.

Chusquea tenuis (hort.)

Chusquea uliginosa

Chusquea tomentosa

Chusquea valdiviensis

Chusquea tenuis (hort.)

Height: 12–20 ft. (4–6 m)?
Diameter: 1 1/2 in. (4 cm) max.?
Light: mostly sunny
Zone 7

The correct botanical name for this cultivated plant is unclear. *Chusquea tenuis* can be a synonym for *C. acuminata*, and *tenuis* sometimes references a form of *C. culeou*. *Chusquea tenuis* is also the botanical name for a unique taxon. Nonetheless, regardless of its correct botanical name, the plant in cultivation in the United States is an attractive one with short branches and upright foliage leaves, characteristics that are more pronounced when the plant is grown in bright sun.

Chusquea tomentosa

Height: 16–30 ft. (5–9 m)
Diameter: 1 1/2 in. (4 cm) max.
Light: partial shade
Zone 9

Indigenous to the montane oak forests of Costa Rica at elevations of 8200 to 9800 ft. (2500 to 2940 m). Prefers slightly drier conditions than some of the other chusqueas of the area, including *C. foliosa* and *C. subtilis*. Grows under the tree canopy, as well as in exposed gaps in the canopy. The culms are erect at the base, then begin to arch and will clamber into trees in the overstory. An attractive bamboo, with tufts of branches and foliage along the culm.

Chusquea uliginosa

Height: 12–30 ft. (4–9 m)
Diameter: 1 in. (2.5 cm) max.
Light: mostly sunny
Zone 7

Grows along the perimeter of seasonal wetlands in its native habitat in southern Chile. It can clamber up to 30 ft. (9 m) high or more into trees. In the landscape, it can be pruned to an attractive, strongly arching habit.

Chusquea valdiviensis

Height: 16–40 ft. (5–12 m)
Diameter: 1 1/2 in. (4 cm) max.
Light: mostly sunny
Zone 7

Native to southern Chile. Can clamber to a height of 40 ft. (12 m) into overstory trees to reach sunlight. It is an aggressive colonizer in disturbed forested areas, often readily overwhelming other foliage. As it grows larger, it becomes less appealing as an ornamental and unsuited for residential gardens.

DENDROCALAMUS

A genus of arborescent Old World tropical bamboos with pachymorph rhizomes and a clumping habit, *Dendrocalamus* comprises 52 known species. Among these are the world's largest bamboos, several reaching heights of 100 ft. (30 m) or more. Culms may be up to 1 ft. (30 cm) in diameter. The large leaves are up to 20 in. (50 cm) long and 4 in. (10 cm) wide in some species.

Although similar to *Bambusa*, *Dendrocalamus* does not include species with spiny branches. Some bambusa are moderately cold tolerant, but dendrocalamus require a semitropical or tropical environment. Most *Dendrocalamus* species are associated with areas of high rainfall or montane habitats, but *D. strictus* is a prominent exception, inhabiting lowlands and drier regions.

Dendrocalamus asper

Height: 40–100 ft. (12–30 m)
Diameter: 8 in. (20 cm) max.
Light: full sun
Zone 10

Dendrocalamus asper

Dendrocalamus asper 'Nubian Queen'

Dendrocalamus brandisii

An attractive ornamental with a striking presence in the landscape. Native to Southeast Asia and widely cultivated throughout tropical Asia. Its culms are used for paper pulp and construction. It is also cultivated for its large and excellent tasting shoots. A single shoot can weigh up to 16 lb. (7.2 kg) or more.

'Betung Hitam'. Culms turn brown, then a striking black with age.

'Nubian Queen'. A seed selection with dark culms.

Dendrocalamus brandisii

Height: 40–100 ft. (12–30 m)
Diameter: 8 in. (20 cm) max.
Light: full sun
Zone 10
Native to India and Southeast Asia. Among the world's largest bamboos. The lower nodes are branchless, but may have pronounced aerial roots. The thick-walled culms are used in construction. The new shoots are choice for eating.

Dendrocalamus giganteus, new shoot and culms.

Dendrocalamus giganteus, with tropical and other hot-climate plants.

'Black'. Striking black culms dry to dark brown. Choice for furniture.

Variegated. An unnamed cultivar with variegated leaves.

Dendrocalamus giganteus

Height: 45–115 ft. (14–35 m)
Diameter: 12 in. (30 cm) max.
Light: full sun
Zone 10

Indigenous to India, Burma, and Thailand, it is also cultivated in China's Yunnan Province and in Taiwan. Though a few bamboos approach its size, *Dendrocalamus giganteus* is likely the world's largest bamboo. Lower nodes may be branchless for 40 ft. (12 m) or more. Leaves grow up to 20 in. (50 cm) long and 4 in. (10 cm) wide.

The young shoots are suitable for the table, and its culms are used for paper manufacturing, building construction, boat masts, furniture, buckets, water pitchers, vases, and other crafts.

Variegated. An unnamed cultivar with sporadic leaf variegation.

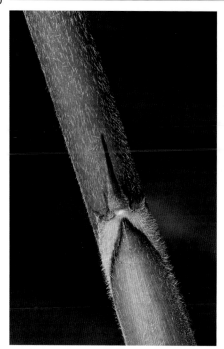

Dendrocalamus hamiltonii

Dendrocalamus latiflorus 'Mei-nung'

Dendrocalamus hamiltonii
Height: 35–80 ft. (10.5–24 m)
Diameter: 7 in. (18 cm) max.
Light: full sun
Zone 10
From the northeast Himalayas. Culms sometimes erect but often curved or arching and pendulous. Lower nodes are bare of branches. Upper nodes branch thickly, with numerous large leaves up to 15 in. (38 cm) long. The young shoots are quite suitable for the table.

Dendrocalamus latiflorus
Height: 35–80 ft. (10.5–24 m)
Diameter: 10 in. (25 cm) max.
Light: full sun
Zone 10
Native to southern China. The upper nodes have large masses of very large dark green leaves up to 16 in. (40 cm) long and 4 in. (10 cm) wide. The young shoots are delicious, and it is one of the more important bamboos for shoot production. In southern China and Taiwan, shoots average 9 lb. (4 kg) each.

'Mei-nung'. Culms and branches are light green, striped with dark green. Leaves have occasional yellow stripes.

Dendrocalamus minor
Height: 12–26 ft. (4–7.8 m)
Diameter: 2¼ in. (6 cm) max.
Light: full sun
Zone 10
Native to China's Guangdong, Guangxi, and Guizhou Provinces. One of the smaller members of the genus and an attractive plant for smaller garden spaces. Mature specimens are erect and branchless near the base with drooping branches on the upper portion.

'Amoenus'. Yellow-green culms with green stripes.

Dendrocalamus minor

Dendrocalamus strictus

Dendrocalamus strictus
Male bamboo
Height: 30–60 ft. (9–18 m)
Diameter: 5 in. (13 cm) max.
Light: full sun
Zone 10

India's most common bamboo. Great beauty is not one of its attributes, but it is a rugged plant, tolerating drought and low humidity. The lower portion of the thick-walled culms is sometimes nearly solid. In India, this bamboo is extensively cultivated for paper pulp.

DREPANOSTACHYUM

Drepanostachyum is a genus of somewhat tender, montane bamboos with pachymorph rhizome systems and a clumping habit. They primarily inhabit elevations of 3300 to 7200 ft. (1000 to 2200 m) in the dry semitropical forests of the Himalayas.

In its native habitats, *Drepanostachyum* does not survive below about 1600 ft. (500 m), where maximum temperatures can reach 104°F (40°C). Above 6100 ft. (1850 m), *Himalayacalamus*, another genus of Himalayan montane bamboos, becomes increasingly prominent.

The two genera are frequently confused and some of the species have long been interchangeably labeled in the nursery trade. Among the distinguishing characteristics, *Himalayacalamus* has a dominant branch, while *Drepanostachyum* has generally equal branches. On a mature *Drepanostachyum* plant, each node has around 25 branches in a new culm's first year and as many as 70 branches in subsequent years.

Drepanostachyum shoots are very bitter and are not suited for the table. The genus is useful as forage or pasture for animals and, despite the somewhat swollen nodes, as weaving material. In the main, however, most species are not widely cultivated except as ornamentals.

Like most montane bamboos, drepanostachyum are not suited to climates with warm soils and hot summer nights.

Drepanostachyum khasianum
Height: 8–16 ft. (2.4–5 m)
Diameter: 1/2 in. (1.25 cm) max.
Light: partial shade
Zone 9

In its natural environment, *Drepanostachyum khasianum* is heavily browsed and is most often encountered as a scruffy scrub plant less than 10 ft. (3 m) tall. Protected, it is an attractive, rather tender, mountain bamboo with dark green leaves that are relatively large for a montane bamboo. The dark green new culms are covered with waxy powder. In Europe, the name has

Drepanostachyum khasianum

sometimes been misapplied to other species. The plants in general circulation in the United States appear to be correctly named.

FARGESIA

Clumping bamboos with pachymorph rhizomes are commonly associated with semitropical or tropical bamboos with little cold tolerance, but some species of *Fargesia* are among the most cold hardy of all bamboos. Both *F. nitida* and *F. murielae*, for example, can withstand temperature drops to −20°F (−29°C) without leaf damage. These species have been growing successfully in Norway for more than 30 years, and *F. nitida* has survived winters as far north as Tromsø, Norway, at nearly latitude 70°N, well into the Arctic Circle.

The genus *Fargesia* comprises approximately 80 species, though some now belong in the recently identified genus *Borinda*. They are na-tive to the alpine conifer forests of western and southwestern China, where the towering mountains and terrain create isolated pockets and unique environments. The entire population of some species may exist on a single mountain, or even on a single mountain slope.

Fargesias are small to medium-sized bamboos that exhibit a typical montane bamboo form, with numerous branches and delicate leaves on slender arching culms—more bushlike than arborescent. All are very cold tolerant, but are not tolerant of summer heat, strong afternoon sunlight, warm soils, or drought conditions.

In a landscape or other controlled environment, shade and water can be provided, but ensuring moderate summer temperatures is more of a problem. Most fargesias are not the best choice in climates where the severe cold temperatures of winter are matched by the intense heat of summer.

Fargesia apicirubens type form (left) and 'White Dragon' (right)

Fargesia apicirubens

Fargesia denudata

Fargesia apicirubens

Height: 8–16 ft. (2.4–5 m)
Diameter: $^3/_4$ in. (2 cm) max.
Light: partial shade
Zone 6

Native to China at elevations above 6000 ft. (1800 m). The dense, dark green foliage leaves do not curl in the sun and heat like many others of the genus. Very attractive, with a strongly weeping habit. Many of the plants in circulation have been propagated from seedlings grown in the late 1980s or early 1990s. Some clones are more vigorous than others. Plants in circulation were previously incorrectly identified as *Fargesia dracocephala*.

'White Dragon'. White variegated leaves. Variegation most pronounced on new spring growth. The only variegated *Fargesia* in cultivation. Some culms may revert to green and require removal to preserve the variegated effect. Smaller and less vigorous than primary form.

Fargesia denudata

Height: 10–16 ft. (3–5 m)
Diameter: $^1/_2$ in. (1.25 cm) max.
Light: partial shade
Zone 7

From northern Sichuan and southern Gansu, China, at elevations of 6235 to 10,000 ft. (1900 to 3000 m). Similar in appearance to the more familiar *Fargesia murielae*, but the leaves are smaller. The branches are relatively short, allowing the arching culms to stand out individually rather than simply being a part of a foliage mass.

Fargesia dracocephala 'Rufa'

Height: 6–10 ft. (1.8–3 m)
Diameter: $^1/_2$ in. (1.25 cm) max.
Light: partial shade
Zone 6

From northern Sichuan, southern Shaanxi, western Hubei, and southern Gansu, China, at elevations

Fargesia dracocephala 'Rufa'

Fargesia murielae

of 5000 to 7200 ft. (1500 to 2200 m). One of the shorter *Fargesia* and earliest shooting in the spring. It is a major food source for the giant panda.

Fargesia murielae
Umbrella bamboo
Height: 8–15 ft. (2.4–4.6 m)
Diameter: 1/2 in. (1.25 cm) max.
Light: mostly shade
Zone 5
One of the world's most winter hardy bamboos. The green culms bear masses of delicate pea-green leaves. In a clump, the upper portion of the culms arch in a manner reminiscent of an umbrella's shape, thus the plant's common name, umbrella bamboo. Like most fargesias, it needs some shade and a wide space to display its airy, arching mass of foliage.

Native to China at elevations of up to over 10,000 ft. (3000 m), it is a food source for the giant panda. It was collected in China's Hubei Province in 1907 by the famous British plant collector Ernest H. Wilson and named after his daughter, Muriel.

We now have numerous choices of high-altitude Asian montane bamboos, but *Fargesia murielae* remains a prime candidate, particular where winter hardiness is a concern.

Fargesia nitida
Fountain bamboo
Height: 8–12 ft. (2.4–4 m)
Diameter: 1/2 in. (1.25 cm) max.
Light: mostly shade
Zone 5
Native to Gansu, Ningxia, Qinghai, and Sichuan, China, at elevations of 6235 to 10,000 ft. (1900 to 3000 m). Along with *Fargesia murielae*, *F. nitida* is one of the world's most winter hardy bamboos, and a choice ornamental.

The dark red-purple or dark brown-purple of the culms becomes more pronounced with some sun exposure, setting off the masses of delicate dark green leaves. Young culms are coated with a blue-white waxy powder. New shoots are branchless in the first season, branching in the second year.

Fargesia nitida 'Nymphenburg'

Fargesia nitida 'Juizhaigou'

Fargesia robusta

Fargesia nitida

The culms are more upright than those of *Fargesia murielae*, giving the clump more of a fountain shape than an umbrella shape. In China, this species is one of the food plants for the giant panda.

The older generation of this species from the 1880s yielded many cultivars, but all have gone or will go to seed. New generation cultivars are beginning to appear.

'Juizhaigou'. New culms turn red when exposed to sun, turning soft orangey yellow with age. Small delicate leaves.

'Nymphenburg'. Older generation, but some have not yet flowered. Narrower leaves and more arching culms than the primary form.

Fargesia robusta
Height: 12–20 ft. (4–6 m)
Diameter: 1 in. (2.5 cm) max.
Light: mostly sunny
Zone 6

Fargesia robusta 'Wolong'

Fargesia sp. 'Scabrida', new culms still sheathed by their culm leaves.

Native to western Sichuan, China, at elevations of 5580 to 9200 ft. (1700 to 2800 m) and an important food source for the giant panda. Living up to its species name, it is among the larger, upright, and vigorous of the genus. It shoots early in the spring. The semi-persistent culm leaves form an appealing patterned look on the new culms.

The culms are used for weaving and walking sticks in China, and the shoots are harvested for the table. Although it is much more tolerant of sun than most of the genus, it will need more shade in warmer regions and will be less tall and vigorous if exposed to excessive sun and heat.

'Campbell'. Smaller leaves and more upright.
'Wolong'. More vigorous with larger leaves.

Fargesia sp. 'Scabrida'
Height: 8–14 ft. (2.4–4.3 m)
Diameter: ¾ in. (2 cm) max.
Light: mostly sunny
Zone 6

Collected in the mountains of northern Sichuan, China, at an elevation of over 8500 ft. (2600 m), the species of this attractive plant has not yet been determined. Gunmetal blue to purplish culms turn olive green as they age. Culm and branch sheaths sometimes take on a striking rusty-orange coloration, clinging for a time before dropping. The leaves are dark green. Like *Fargesia robusta*, it is among the more upright and sun tolerant of the genus.

Fargesia utilis
Height: 10–20 ft. (3–6 m)
Diameter: ¾ in. (2 cm) max.
Light: mostly sunny
Zone 7
From northeastern Yunnan, China, at elevations of 8900 to 12,000 ft. (2700 to 3700 m). On mature plants, masses of small leaves weigh heavily on the culms, arching them outward and nearly

Fargesia utilis

Fargesia utilis, new shoots.

to the ground. The portions of new culms protruding from the foliage mass turn burgundy red in the sun. An impressive foliage plume where ample space is available, but not a plant for smaller gardens.

GIGANTOCHLOA

Native to Asia and the Pacific Islands, *Gigantochloa* is a genus of giant, tropical, clumping bamboos with pachymorph rhizomes. *Gigantochloa* species generally resemble *Bambusa* species. Unlike many other tropical bamboos, *Gigantochloa* does not generally die after flowering, but may partially flower on an irregular basis, or not flower at all.

It has been suggested that many of the *Gigantochloa* forms in cultivation in Indonesia today are the result of selection, cultivation, and vegetative propagation of elite hybrid forms dating back thousands of years ago.

There are some 37 known species, but it has been estimated that there may be as many as 200 *Gigantochloa* forms.

Gigantochloa apus

Height: 30–65 ft. (9–20 m)
Diameter: 4 in. (10 cm) max.
Light: full sun
Zone 10

Native to Java, *Gigantochloa apus* is an exceptionally strong bamboo, both as a whole culm and split for woven work. The strong culms taper very little and are used for roof rafters. The bitter shoots are buried in the mud for several days before being cooked and eaten. The leaves are up to 15 in. (38 cm) long and 2½ in. (6.3 cm) wide. *Gigantochloa apus* was introduced into the United States in about 1932, and subsequently established in other New World locations, including Puerto Rico and Nicaragua.

Gigantochloa atroviolacea

Height: 25–55 ft. (7.6–17 m)
Diameter: 3¾ in. (9.5 cm) max.
Light: full sun
Zone 10

A highly attractive ornamental bamboo from Java and Sumatra. The young culms are initially dark green, turning rapidly to deep brown-black or deep purple-black. The culm leaves drop quickly to ensure that the attractive new culms are visually unencumbered. Lower nodes may have aerial roots.

The cured culms retain their black color and are used for building and furniture construction, musical instruments, and other craft items. The shoots are edible.

This species is often mistaken for *Bambusa lako*, which it closely resembles. The culms of *B. lako* have a shiny surface, however, whereas those of *G. atroviolacea* have more of a matt finish.

Gigantochloa pseudoarundinacea

Height: 25–100 ft. (7.6–30 m)
Diameter: 5 in. (13 cm) max.
Light: full sun
Zone 10

Gigantochloa apus

Gigantochloa atroviolacea

This bamboo was introduced into the United States and other parts of the New World as *Gigantochloa verticillata*, but many different species in the genus were erroneously included under that name. *Gigantochloa pseudoarundinacea* has been separated from that group and given its own identity. It has likely been in cultivation for thousands of years, and reportedly there are a number of variations with distinct characteristics, but all have striped culms and are very attractive ornamentals. Although potentially among the tallest timber bamboos, *G. pseudoarundinacea* seldom approaches its maximum height and is typically much smaller. The culms are strong, straight, and easily worked, and the shoots are good tasting.

GUADUA

Most New World bamboos are relatively small, but some species of *Guadua* rival the largest of the Old World bamboos. *Guadua* consists of approximately 24 described species and a few more undescribed species. They range from various vining types to the giant South American species for which the genus is noted.

Unlike some *Bambusa*, *Guadua* species are generally intolerant of cold. They generally have thorny basal branches. The internodes may contain water, suggesting that the water may be stored and reused during dry periods. The culm leaves are deciduous, quickly revealing the new culm.

The natural habitat ranges from sea level to 7200 ft. (2200 m), from Mexico through Uruguay and Argentina, excluding Chile. It comprises the most extensive bamboo forests of any New World bamboo genus, covering vast areas in the Brazilian Amazon and Peru alone.

Most bamboos with pachymorph rhizome systems have a clumping habit, but some tropical bamboos, such as species of *Guadua*, are exceptions. The long-necked rhizomes of some species may extend some 20 ft. (6 m) or more before turning upward into a new culm, easily outdistancing many running bamboos with leptomorph rhizome systems. In marginal, nontropical climates, however, their growth is far less aggressively running.

Guadua aculeata
Height: 30–70 ft. (9–21 m)?
Diameter: 4 in. (10 cm) max.?
Light: full sun
Zone 10
Native to southern Mexico and Central America, *Guadua aculeata* has been considered a form of *G. angustifolia*, but distinctive characteristics in its inflorescence show that it is a separate species. The culms are useful in construction, though other *Guadua* species with superior culm wood are generally preferred.

Guadua amplexifolia
Height: 30–60 ft. (9–18 m)
Diameter: 4 in. (10 cm) max.
Light: full sun
Zone 10
Guadua amplexifolia has a more pronounced arching habit than other large *Guadua* species. Thorniness varies, but examples from the more northerly reaches of its range in southern Mexico are less thorny or without thorns. The culm internodes are short. Lower culm leaves are persistent, but upper culm leaves rapidly drop away.

Guadua angustifolia
Height: 50–100 ft. (15–30 m)
Diameter: 9 in. (22 cm) max.
Light: full sun
Zone 10
Largest of all the New World bamboos. Native to northeastern South America, it is prominent in Colombia and Ecuador, where it is known, respectively, as *guadua* and *caña brava*. China has its remarkable moso forests; South America has its guaduales, expanses of land dominated by species of *Guadua*, prominent among them *G. angustifolia*.

The species thrives in a fairly broad elevation range, from sea level to 5900 ft. (1770 m). It grows best within a temperature range of 63 to 75°F (17 to 24°C)—clearly not a bamboo that thrives on frosty conditions. Nor is it a bamboo for dry conditions, thriving in natural habitats with an annual precipitation ranging from 80 to 240 in. (2000 to 6000 mm) a year.

Gigantochloa pseudoarundinacea

Guadua amplexifolia, with prominent new thorns.

Guadua aculeata

Guadua angustifolia

It is one of the world's finest structural bamboos, if not the finest. The culms are very strong and easily worked. It is used by indigenous peoples in construction of modest homes, as well as in multimillion-dollar architectural masterpieces.

Most tropical bamboos are chronically subject to insect attack and rot, but *Guadua angustifolia*, even when untreated, is highly resistant. Documented accounts have demonstrated that its longevity is greater than that of hardwoods used alongside it.

It is quite thorny. On a large scale in a hot tropical environment with ample moisture, it has greatly elongated rhizome necks and is a vigorous runner, but it is much more restrained in the few American and European climates able to grow it.

'Bicolor'. Culms have yellow and green striping.

'Less Thorny'. Fewer and smaller thorns.

Guadua paniculata

Height: 20–40 ft. (6–12 m)
Diameter: 2¾ in. (7 cm) max.
Light: full sun
Zone 10

From Mexico to Brazil. Adapted to seasonally dry conditions. Somewhat resembling *Otatea*. Thorny, with long-necked rhizomes, it sometimes dominates hillsides in its native environment.

HIBANOBAMBUSA

The name *Hibanobambusa* means "bamboo growing on Mount Hiba." This single-species genus originated in the wild from a crossing of a *Sasa* bamboo and a *Phyllostachys* bamboo sometime around the end of the 19th century or beginning of the 20th century.

Hibanobambusa flowered in the early 1970s, but apparently few seeds were produced and none proved viable. The flowers are reportedly

Guadua paniculata

Hibanobambusa tranquillans 'Shiroshima'

Hibanobambusa tranquillans 'Shiroshima', accenting a pathway through the garden.

similar to those of *Phyllostachys*, but they usually have six stamens, as in *Sasa*.

Hibanobambusa has a leptomorph rhizome and a running habit. The culm leaves drop away rapidly, as with *Phyllostachys*, but each node generally bears only one branch (or occasionally two or three branches after the first year). Like *Sasa*, the leaves are large.

Hibanobambusa tranquillans

Height: 6–16 ft. (1.8–5 m)
Diameter: 1 1/4 in. (3.2 cm) max.
Light: mostly sunny
Zone 7
Sharing some of the overt characteristics of its parents, *Hibanobambusa tranquillans* has the larger leaves of a *Sasa*, up to 10 in. (25 cm) long

and 1 1/4 in. (3.2 cm) wide, and the deciduous culm leaves characteristic of *Phyllostachys*. It tolerates full sun, but also grows well in partial shade.

'Shiroshima'. Strongly variegated, white-striped leaves. When grown in strong sun, some of the leaves may have purple tones in the variegation. An attractive ornamental that is far more widely grown than the green form.

HIMALAYACALAMUS

Himalayacalamus is a genus of marginally hardy montane bamboos with pachymorph rhizomes and a clumping habit that grow up to 30 ft. (9 m) tall. Species are found at elevations of 6100 to 9200 ft. (1850 to 2800 m) in the cool, broad-leaved forests of the Himalayas.

Slender culms, profuse with fine branches and delicate leaves, are the hallmark of these attractive bamboos. In the first year of culm growth, each node has about 15 branches. In subsequent years, a node may have up to 40 branches.

Himalayacalamus is frequently confused with *Drepanostachyum*, and some of the species have been mistakenly interchangeably labeled in the nursery trade, exacerbating and perpetuating the problem. *Himalayacalamus* has a dominant branch, while *Drepanostachyum* has generally equal branches. In its natural environment, *Himalayacalamus* is typically found

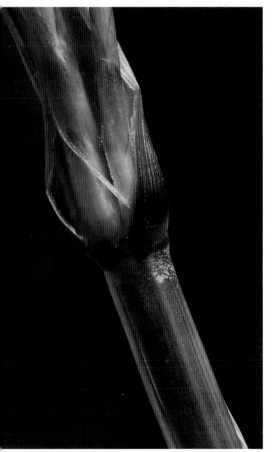

Himalayacalamus falconeri 'Damarapa', branches emerging from a new culm.

at higher elevations than *Drepanostachyum*, and is more cold tolerant, but less tolerant of drought. The culms of some *Himalayacalamus* species are slightly larger, reaching 2 in. (5 cm), versus a maximum of 1¼ in. (3.2 cm) for *Drepanostachyum*.

Himalayacalamus plants are useful as forage, pasture for animals, and as weaving material. The new shoots of many species are excellent for the table.

Like most montane bamboos, himalayacalamus are intolerant of hot nights and warm soils and are generally not suited to climates such as the U.S. Southeast.

Himalayacalamus falconeri

Height: 12–30 ft. (4–9 m)
Diameter: 2 in. (5 cm) max.
Light: partial shade
Zone 8

In its native environment, *Himalayacalamus falconeri* is found at relatively high elevations, ranging from 6600 to 8200 ft. (2000 to 2500 m). The shoots are edible and can be found for sale in the markets of Katmandu. The relatively large, flexible culms make excellent weaving material.

'Damarapa' (candy-stripe bamboo). A striking ornamental, displaying culms with green and yellow stripes that change to lavender, red, orange, and pink tones, characteristics enhanced by exposure to sun and nighttime cooling. Somewhat temperamental to grow, but worth the effort in suitable climates. Previously misidentified in the nursery trade as *Drepanostachyum hookerianum*.

Himalayacalamus hookerianus
Blue bamboo

Height: 12–20 ft. (4–6 m)
Diameter: 1 in. (2.5 cm) max.
Light: mostly shade
Zone 8

New culms are a striking blue color with purple overtones, complemented by a profusion of small delicate leaves. In subsequent years, the culm coloration ranges from yellow-green to purple-red. The lower nodes are free of branches, and the internodes are long, contributing to the desirability of the culms for weaving.

In its natural environment, *Himalayacalamus hookerianus* is an understory plant. Sheltered by the forest canopy that mitigates the harshness of wind and cold, it can prosper in spite of its marginal hardiness.

Named after Sir Joseph Hooker, who found the bamboo in flower in 1848 on an approach to a mountain pass in Sikkim. Formerly misidentified in the garden trade as *Drepanostachyum falcatum*.

Himalayacalamus planatus

Height: 10–20 ft. (3–6 m)
Diameter: ½ in. (1.25 cm) max.
Light: partial shade
Zone 8

Indigenous to Nepal, *Himalayacalamus planatus* had belonged within *H. asper* but is now recognized as a separate species. The name *planatus* references the culm nodes that are level with the internodes with virtually no prominence. In the United States, *H. planatus* has been circulated in the nursery trade as *H. asper* and prior to that was misidentified as *Neomicrocalamus microphyllus*.

Himalayacalamus hookerianus

Himalayacalamus planatus

Himalayacalamus planatus

Himalayacalamus porcatus

Regardless of the nomenclatural confusion, this bamboo is among the more delicate of the Himalayan montane bamboos. A profusion of delicate leaves are supported by slender culms that remain green in the shade but turn dark reddish purple with sun exposure. A mature clump is widely arching from weight of the leaves on the slender culms.

The flexible culms are often used for weaving, although when available, other *Himalayacalamus* species with longer internodes are used in preference.

Himalayacalamus porcatus

Height: 10–20 ft. (3–6 m)
Diameter: 1 in. (2.5 cm) max.
Light: partial shade
Zone 8
Native to central Nepal at elevations of 6600 to 7500 ft. (2000 to 2300 m). Unique within *Himalayacalamus*, it has finely ridged internodes. New culms have a light blue to blue-green color. Unlike most montane bamboos, it is not well-suited to weaving, as its culms are brittle, and they are sharp-edged when split.

INDOCALAMUS

Somewhat similar to *Sasa*, *Indocalamus* is a genus of broad-leaved bamboos usually with a single main branch per node. Near the top of the culm, the nodes may have up to three branches.

Unlike *Sasa*, the culm nodes are unswollen, and the leaves typically have a greater length-to-width ratio—a length of more than four times their width in *Indocalamus*, but frequently less than four times their width in *Sasa*. Also unlike *Sasa*, *Indocalamus* suffers little from withering of the leaf tips or leaf margins, thus sometimes offering a brighter, fresher look.

Indocalamus culm leaf sheaths are persistent and usually shorter than the internodes. The diameter of the branches is nearly the same as the diameter of the culm.

The approximately 35 known species of *Indocalamus* have leptomorph rhizome systems and a strongly running habit. Most prefer some shade and are quite cold hardy.

Indocalamus latifolius

Height: 5–10 ft. (1.5–3 m)
Diameter: $^3/_8$ in. (1 cm) max.
Light: partial shade
Zone 6

Native to central and eastern China. The culms are used for making chopsticks, brushes, and pens. The leaves are up to 15 in. (38 cm) long and 3 in. (7.5 cm) wide, and are used to make mats, to line hats, or for wrapping food. In the landscape, it makes a large, attractive, upright bush or hedge.

Indocalamus latifolius

Indocalamus sp. 'Hamadae'

Height: 5–15 ft. (1.5–4.6 m)
Diameter: ⅝ in. (1.5 cm) max.
Light: partial shade
Zone 6

Native to Kyushu, Japan. Large tropical-looking leaves similar to the Chinese *Indocalamus tessellatus*, but potentially taller with a denser leaf canopy, often having three leaves per branch. The large leaves were once commonly used for wrapping rice.

Indocalamus sp. 'Solidus'

Height: 3–8 ft. (0.9–2.4 m)
Diameter: ⅜ in. (1 cm) max.
Light: partial shade
Zone 6

At up to 10 in. (25 cm) long, the leaves are smaller and less drooping than the more widely known species of the genus. The plant is named for its culm internodes, which are solid rather than hollow.

Indocalamus sp. 'Solidus'

Indocalamus sp. 'Hamadae'

Indocalamus tessellatus

Indocalamus tessellatus

Height: 3–10 ft. (0.9–3 m)
Diameter: ³⁄₈ in. (1 cm) max.
Light: partial shade to full sun
Zone 5

Native to Hunan, China. Leaves are up to 2 ft. (60 cm) long and 4 in. (10 cm) wide, the largest leaves of any temperate-climate bamboo. The large drooping leaves obscure the culms and branches, giving the plant more of a mounded bush appearance than some of the other members of the genus. Rarely reaches maximum possible height. Despite the tropical look of its foliage, this species is very hardy, and it grows well in containers. Its large leaves are used for making mats and for wrapping food.

Nastus elatus

NASTUS

Nastus is a genus of some 24 species of clumping bamboos with pachymorph rhizomes. They are distributed from Madagascar through Indonesia, Papua New Guinea, to the Solomon Islands. Some species are arborescent and others are clambering or climbing.

Nastus elatus

Height: 30–60 ft. (9–18 m)
Diameter: 4 in. (10 cm) max.
Light: full sun
Zone 10

From the highlands of Papua New Guinea. Erect elegant clumps with long narrow light green leaves drooping gracefully from nodding upper branches. New culms are bright green, turning yellowish with age. New shoots are excellent for the table. Like most tropicals it needs heat and humidity to grow well.

OLMECA

Indigenous to southern Mexico, *Olmeca* is named after the Olmecs, an ancient civilization predating the Mayas. The genus consists of two species, *O. recta* and *O. reflexa*.

Olmecas have pachymorph rhizomes, but hardly a clumping habit. Their rhizome necks may extend up to 26 ft. (7.8 m) before turning upward to form a culm. The branching habit is also somewhat unusual. A single branch may form at each node, but then branch no further. Also relatively uncommon for bamboos, *Olmeca* produces fleshy fruits when it flowers.

Olmeca recta

Height: 20–45 ft. (6–14 m)
Diameter: 2 in. (5 cm) max.
Light: mostly sunny
Zone 10

Indigenous to the wet lowland forests of southern Mexico at elevations from sea level to 2600 ft (800 m). The culms are hollow and thin walled, covered by hard, persistent culm leaves. Branching begins at about 10 ft. (3 m) above the ground, and the foliage leaves have a palmlike appearance. In its native environment, *Olmeca recta* forms dense stands known locally as *jimbales*.

OTATEA

Otatea is a New World genus of subtropical or tropical bamboos with pachymorph rhizomes and a clumping habit. They are more drought resistant than most New World bamboos.

Their habitat includes seasonally dry areas along the Pacific Coast of Mexico and Central America, where the bamboos share territory with cacti and agaves. Given the limestone soils typical of their habitat, otateas prefer less acidic soils than most bamboos. The genus name is a derivative of *otate*, the name used by the Nahuatl Indians of central Mexico.

Otatea acuminata

Height: 4–20 ft. (1.2–6 m)
Diameter: 1½ in. (4 cm) max.
Light: mostly sunny
Zones 9 to 10

Olmeca recta

Native to Northeastern Mexico through Honduras in Central America. The culm leaves persist on the lower portions of the culm. Each node typically has three similarly sized branches. The species varies in form, and two subspecies and additional cultivars are recognized.

Subsp. *acuminata*. Native to the hot lowlands of Mexico, and among the earliest cultivated New World bamboos. The slender arching culms are covered with delicate, feathery masses of leaves. The culms are used to make baskets, corrals, furniture, and toys, and also incorporated into the walls, doors, and ceilings of buildings. It is particularly desirable as roofing material, since

Otatea acuminata subsp. aztecorum, in flower and setting seed.

Otatea acuminata 'Michoacán'

it is more resistant than other bamboos to rot, fungi, and insects.

Subsp. *aztecorum*. Larger and more cold-hardy than subsp. *acuminata*. Its masses of long, narrow, drooping, light green leaves nearly obscure the culms, giving the appearance of a cascading fountain. Its rhizome necks are relatively long, so the clumps are more open with culms spaced up to 2 ft. (60 cm) apart in large mature clumps grown in a hot climate.

Subsp. *aztecorum* 'Dwarf'. A dwarf form, growing much smaller than the primary form to a reported height of 4 ft. (1.2 m) or less.

'Michoacán'. Darker culms. The culm leaves are more persistent, and the foliage leaves are less pliant, giving this cultivar a less delicate appearance.

Otatea fimbriata

Height: 8–14 ft. (2.4–4.3 m)
Diameter: ¾ in. (2 cm) max.
Light: mostly sunny
Zone 9

Otatea fimbriata

Distributed from Mexico to northern Columbia. Larger leaves than the other members of the genus, measuring up to 12 in. (30 cm) long and ³⁄₄ in. (2 cm) wide.

OXYTENANTHERA
Native to the savanna woodlands of tropical Africa. *Oxytenanthera* species have pachymorph rhizome systems and a clumping habit.

Oxytenanthera braunii
Wine bamboo
Height: 15–30 ft. (4.6–9 m)
Diameter: 4 in. (10 cm) max.
Light: full sun
Zone 10
The new shoots of *Oxytenanthera braunii* exude sap for many weeks after being topped. In Tanzania, plants are topped at a height of roughly 3 ft. (90 cm), and the sap is collected and fermented into a winelike beverage called *ulanzi*, hence the common name wine bamboo. A single culm yields about 2³⁄₄ gallons (10 liters) of sap. Reports of the drink's merit range from tasty to quite foul.

PHYLLOSTACHYS
Phyllostachys is a large genus of approximately 75 species and more than 200 varieties and forms. The species are widely distributed in the wild, in the temperate and semitropical areas of eastern Asia, from sea level up to 12,000 ft. (3700 m). *Phyllostachys* is the most northerly of all the giant arborescent bamboos.

Eastern China appears to be the center of distribution. As with many species that have long been cultivated, the original, natural pattern of distribution of *Phyllostachys* is unclear, and some distribution is likely to have occurred via human migration in very early times.

Nearly all *Phyllostachys* species can be found in China, though *P. humilis* is an exception. Cultivated in Japan, *P. humilis* is assumed to have originated in China, but has not yet been recorded there.

An impressive genus, *Phyllostachys* comprises many of the world's most beautiful, and eco-

Oxytenanthera braunii

nomically important, hardy bamboos. In China and Japan, it is the principal source of edible bamboo shoots, paper pulp, craftwork, and timber. In established forests, some species can reach a height of more than 90 ft. (27 m) and a diameter of 7 in. (18 cm).

Although some *Phyllostachys* are huge plants with rapidly spreading leptomorph rhizomes, new rhizomes grow very close to the soil surface. As a result, the plant's spread can be readily controlled with barriers or rhizome pruning more easily than other genera of leptomorph bamboos that may be much smaller, but have more rampant and deeper running rhizomes.

Members of this genus are readily identifiable by a pronounced sulcus (groove) that runs the length of the internode on the branching side. The branch buds, already prominent, are pressed against the emerging internode by the tightly wrapped culm leaf sheaths, creating the sulcus as the internode elongates. On a *Phyllostachys* culm, only the lowermost internodes that emerge from branchless nodes are absent a sulcus.

Some other bamboo genera, such as *Semiarundinaria*, have a partial sulcus, but a pronounced sulcus running the full length of the internode is unique to *Phyllostachys*. It is, perhaps, the most readily identifiable bamboo genus. In some forms and cultivars, the sulcus is a different color than the rest of the culm, typically yellow on a green culm or green on a yellow culm.

Except for the lower nodes of older culms where the branch buds may remain dormant, branch development and emergence in *Phyllostachys* begins concurrently with the growth of the culm. The lowest nodes on the culm may have solitary branches, but the typical branching pattern is two major, but unequally sized branches at each node. Occasionally, a third, much smaller branch may develop between the two principal branches.

The culms and branches encompass a broad range of colors and surface finishes, including lime green, sulfur green, sulfur yellow, bluish green, chocolate, olive, straw yellow, green and yellow striped, shiny and waxy, velvety, matt finished, or white powdered. The coloration and patterns of *Phyllostachys* culm leaf sheaths are

Some leaves of this *Phyllostachys* plant are withering and falling away, making way for new branchlets.

Characteristic of the genus *Phyllostachys*, the culm leaves are rapidly deciduous, clinging only briefly at the edge of the sheath base.

highly distinctive, and they are often an excellent means of readily identifying a species in the field.

The culm and branch leaves are immediately deciduous, dropping from the lower nodes, even as the upper internodes continue their extension. The immediately deciduous nature of *Phyllostachys* culm and branch leaves enhances their appeal in the landscape—not only is a scruffy look avoided, but the visual appeal is enhanced by immediate exposure of the bright fresh look of new culms and branches.

Although, like nearly all bamboos, *Phyllostachys* is evergreen, it replaces its leaves gradually. The replacement is inconspicuous except for the carpet of fallen leaves beneath the plant, which adds to the desirable layer of mulch. The principal leaf fall occurs in the spring. New leaves appear on new twigs, which are generated from lower buds on the existing twigs.

The leaves of *Phyllostachys* are lanceolate and distinctly tessellated. The lower leaves on a twig are somewhat shorter and broader, the upper leaves somewhat longer and narrower. A very young plant often has larger, sometimes much larger, leaves than an older plant of the same species. Older plants, with "normal," smaller leaves and larger culms, begin to assume more of the arborescent stature and beauty for which this genus of giant, hardy, tree grasses is known.

Shoot initiation varies according to local conditions, but generally begins in early to mid spring (March or April) for early shooting species, through late spring to early summer (June or July) for late-shooting species. Some species, such as *Phyllostachys aurea*, exhibit a propensity for continued sporadic shooting throughout the growing season. *Phyllostachys bissetii, P. edulis, P. nuda,* and *P. violascens* are examples of early shooting species. *Phyllostachys bambusoides* and *P. viridis* are examples of late-shooting species.

It is not uncommon for the culms of the earliest shooting species to have completed their vertical growth and be fully branched out before the latest species have even begun shooting. The difference in the time of shooting extends the length of bamboo's most dramatic and interest-ing period, and it extends the season for harvesting shoots for the table.

Phyllostachys angusta
Stone bamboo
Height: 15–25 ft. (4.6–7.6 m)
Diameter: 1½ in. (4 cm) max.
Light: full sun
Zone 6

Introduced from China's Zhejiang Province into the United States in 1917 by plant explorer Frank Meyer. It is among the shorter members of the genus. The culms are straight and strong with a narrow crown of foliage, more reliably remaining

Phyllostachys angusta

Phyllostachys angusta, new culm.

Phyllostachys arcana

upright even in heavy rains or snow. In China, the culms are used for weaving, craftwork, and furniture. The midseason shoots are free of bitterness.

Phyllostachys arcana

Height: 15–27 ft. (4.6–8 m)
Diameter: 1 1/2 in. (4 cm) max.
Light: full sun
Zone 6

The internodes may develop an irregular pattern of black spots with age and exposure to sunlight. The nodes are rather prominent, and the size of the two main branches is more closely equal than is the case in most other species of *Phyllostachys*. Some culms may grow in zigzags. In China, the culms are used for weaving and for handles on farm implements. The early season shoots are harvested for the table.

'Luteosulcata'. Same as the primary form, but with a yellow sulcus.

Phyllostachys atrovaginata
Incense bamboo

Height: 16–35 ft. (5–10.5 m)
Diameter: 2 3/4 in. (7 cm) max.
Light: full sun
Zone 5

The culms have a relatively large diameter in relation to height, so this species is very useful in landscape settings where the substantial look of relatively large bamboo is desired, but not the height that typically accompanies the girth. It establishes and grows rapidly. Like *Phyllostachys heteroclada*, it has air canals in the rhizomes and roots, an adaptation for growing in wet or boggy soils. It gets its common name, incense bamboo, because the surface of the culms has a scent that

*Phyllostachys
arcana
'Luteosulcata'*

Phyllostachys atrovaginata

resembles sandalwood. Rubbing your thumb and index finger along the internode of a young culm exposed to the sun releases the subtle but distinct fragrance. The shoots are good tasting and nearly free from bitterness even when raw.

Phyllostachys aurea
Golden bamboo, fishpole bamboo
Height: 15–27 ft. (4.6–8 m)
Diameter: 1¾ in. (4.4 cm) max.
Light: full sun
Zone 6

The most commonly cultivated bamboo in the United States. The new culms are green, not golden as the name suggests. Older culms that have been exposed to the sun take on more of a golden yellow color, providing the source of inspiration for the name.

Phyllostachys aurea is distinguished by internodes that are often compressed on the lower portions of the culms. The compressed internodes are pleasingly ornamental. They provide a ready-made gripping area, and the bamboo is used for walking sticks and umbrella handles in Asia. In the U.S. South, the use of the culms as fishing poles has given this species the name fishpole bamboo.

When a dense screen close to the ground is needed, Phyllostachys aurea can be more effective than other Phyllostachys, since the density of nodes on the lower portion of the culms also means a greater density of branches. The branches can also be pruned away to expose the ornamental aspects of the compressed internodes.

The culms are straight, stiffly erect, and do not strongly bend toward the light, as is the case with many other bamboos. The midseason shoots are relatively free from bitterness, even when raw. Depending on growing conditions, this species has a tendency for additional, sporadic shooting throughout the growing season.

Phyllostachys aurea is heat, cold, and drought tolerant, and it does well in a container and as a hedge. Most Phyllostachys species grow poorly in subtropical and tropical environments, but P. aurea is more tolerant than most, and it is even grown commercially in Costa Rica for furniture

Phyllostachys aurea, showing the characteristic compressed internodes on the lower portion of the culm. The branches are newly formed.

Phyllostachys aurea 'Dr. Don'

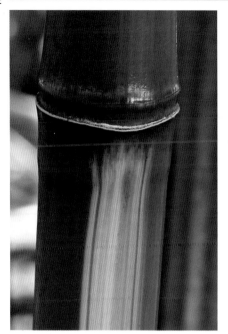

Phyllostachys aurea 'Flavescens-Inversa'

Phyllostachys aurea 'Holochrysa'

Phyllostachys aurea 'Koi'

construction. In hot climates, it can be an aggressive runner.

'Albovariegata'. Variegated white-striped leaves. This cultivar went through a widespread flowering in the late 1990s and most of the surviving plants are no longer variegated.

'Dr. Don'. A new cultivar arising from a seed of the flowering 'Albovariegata'. The new culms have a thicker wax coating than the primary form and are a striking pastel blue. It is not as cold hardy.

'Flavescens-Inversa'. Culms have a yellow sulcus. The compressed lower internodes on some of the culms, combined with the yellow sulcus that alternates from side to side along the internodes, offer a pleasing display of color and texture.

'Holochrysa'. This form of golden bamboo actually reflects the common name of the species. The new culms are pale green, turning progressively to a golden yellow or orange-gold.

'Koi'. The inverse of 'Flavescens-Inversa', the culms of 'Koi' turn yellow, but the sulcus remains green. The leaves may have an occasional white stripe.

'Takemurai'. Lacks the compressed internodes of the primary form and grows somewhat larger.

Phyllostachys aureosulcata
Yellow groove bamboo

Height: 20–45 ft. (6–14 m)
Diameter: 2¼ in. (6 cm) max.
Light: full sun
Zone 5

An excellent, cold hardy ornamental with dark green culms and a yellow sulcus. It is further distinguished by the sharp bending and zigzagging of the lower part of some of the culms. As they are growing, they look at times as if someone had bent or broken them. The culms regain their vertical direction, however, and the grove has an upright habit.

The early midseason shoots are attractive and free of bitterness even when raw. The new culms have a matt finish and are rough to the touch. The crooked lower culms enhance the ornamental appeal, though the bends limit the usefulness of the culm wood, which is, in any case, not of the highest quality.

Phyllostachys aureosulcata is one of the more widely planted ornamental bamboos in China and the United States. First introduced into the United States in 1907 from China's Zhejiang Province, it was widely distributed by the U.S. Department of Agriculture in the 1920s.

This bamboo establishes rapidly and is an excellent choice for climates with cold winters, such as in the U.S. Northeast and Midwest and in Beijing, where Chinese studies have recommended it as a hardy, winter survivor. Although it will not achieve its largest size in cold climates, it is nevertheless an excellent ornamental and screen for cold climate conditions. It is a vigorous grower and runner in warm climates with favorable conditions.

'Alata'. Similar to the primary form, but the sulcus is a conventional green color.

'Aureocaulis'. The culms are entirely yellow, except for occasional green striping on the

Phyllostachys aureosulcata

Phyllostachys aureosulcata 'Alata'

Phyllostachys aureosulcata 'Aureocaulis'

Phyllostachys aureosulcata 'Harbin'

Phyllostachys aureosulcata 'Harbin Inversa'

lowest internodes. The culms and branches often take on rose-red to purple-red tints with exposure to the sun. This characteristic is most evident on young culms and when there is nighttime cooling, making for a striking spring and early summer display.

'Harbin'. Yellow and green striped ribs and grooves that run the length of the internodes.

'Harbin Inversa'. Bright yellow culms with numerous random thin green stripes. New culms may turn orangey-red when exposed to sun. In spite of the name, it is not a sport of 'Harbin' and lacks the longitudinal ribs and grooves.

'Pekinensis'. Similar to and probably synonymous with 'Alata'.

'Spectabilis'. Yellow culms with a green sulcus. New culms and branches often take on rose-red to purple-red tints with exposure to the sun. During shooting, and as the new culm elongates, the attractive culm leaves are further set off by the emerging yellow internodes. Some leaves have light, variegated striping, though this is not a prominent feature.

Phyllostachys aureosulcata 'Spectabilis', showing the characteristic bending of the lower portions of some culms.

Phyllostachys bambusoides
Japanese timber bamboo, madake

Height: 25–72 ft. (7.6–22 m)
Diameter: 6 in. (15 cm) max.
Light: full sun
Zone 7

Native to China, but long cultivated in Japan, where it is the most widely grown timber bamboo. Introduced to Europe in 1866 and to the United States around 1890.

It is one of the latest shooting species of the genus, sometimes not initiating shoots until early summer. The young culms are glossy green. Young plants have long, prominent lower branches. Mature plants are free of branches on the lower nodes.

An emerging culm in a mature grove has been recorded at a growth rate of 47^3⁄$_5$ in. (121 cm) in a single day. Individual culms are among the longest lived, producing new leafy twigs each year for two decades or more. The culms of many other woody bamboos may live for only 5 to 10 years.

Phyllostachys bambusoides is one of the true giant tree grasses. Of the temperate timber bamboos, only *P. edulis* is potentially larger. It must be said, however, that *P. bambusoides* seldom achieves its maximum stated diameter. In the long-established forests of Japan, the culms reportedly average closer to 3^1⁄$_2$ in. (9 cm) in diameter. In the United States, even in established groves, the diameter seldom exceeds 3 in. (7.5 cm).

In Japan, *Phyllostachys bambusoides* and *P. edulis* are primarily distributed in the warmer regions. Japan's third major timber bamboo, *P. nigra* 'Henon', is generally distributed in cooler or more mountainous areas.

The culm wood of *Phyllostachys bambusoides* is ideal for construction—thick, straight, and strong—among the best in the genus and far superior to *P. vivax*, another timber bamboo which it somewhat resembles. The famed shakuhachi flutes are made from the basal portion of a *P. bambusoides* culm. Relative to *P. vivax*, the culms of *P. bambusoides* are straighter and the branches more upright and are produced at lower culm nodes.

Phyllostachys bambusoides is one of the latest shooting of the genus; *P. vivax* shoots relatively early. Unlike *P. vivax*, the shoots of *P. bambusoides* are somewhat bitter, though they are acceptable for the table after parboiling.

Phyllostachys bambusoides establishes and attains size much more slowly than *P. vivax*, and it is not as cold hardy. Because *P. bambusoides* takes longer to establish, it is not ideal when a tall screen is quickly needed, but rewards those who can afford the extra wait.

From a landscaping perspective, *P. bambusoides* and *P. vivax* are similar in appearance. From a commercial or utilization perspective they differ considerably. Most of the cultivar variants of *P. bambusoides* are substantially smaller than the primary form but still impressive.

Phyllostachys bambusoides. The culm leaf is beginning to drop away as the new branches emerge.

Phyllostachys bambusoides

Phyllostachys bambusoides 'Albovariegata'

Phyllostachys bambusoides 'Castillon'

Phyllostachys bambusoides 'Allgold'

'**Albovariegata**'. Striking spring leaf variegation with white and apricot striping. Variegation fades as the season progresses. Much more vigorous, but less continuously variegated than 'Richard Haubrich'.

'**Allgold**'. The new culms are yellow, turning golden with age. The culms are "all gold," without striping, except for an occasional thin green stripe on a lower internode. The coloration of the young culms is quite striking, sometimes appearing translucent in the sunlight. The leaves have occasional cream striping.

'**Castillon**'. New culms are bright straw yellow, with broad, dark green striping in the sulcus. The culms and branches may sometimes take on rosy tints. Some of the leaves have occasional cream pinstripes.

'**Castillon Inversa**'. The "inverse" of 'Castillon', with green culms and a yellow sulcus.

'**Golden Dwarf**'. Small and shrublike with golden leaves and culms.

'**Job's Spots**'. Purple spots in the upper center of the culm leaves.

Phyllostachys bambusoides 'Castillon Inversa'

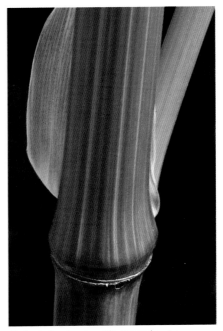

Phyllostachys bambusoides 'Kawadana'

'Kawadana'. Culms have fine gold pinstriping. Leaves lightly striped with gold. The striping and coloration are sometimes muted but are impressive at their best.

'Marliac'. Wrinkled culms formed by many small longitudinal grooves around the circumference of the culm, running the length of each internode. An unusual ornamental that is of more merit when the culms are larger. The culms are used in craftwork.

'Ribleaf'. The leaves are shorter and wider and ribbed along the veins.

'Richard Haubrich'. Heavily variegated leaves with cream and apricot coloration. Far smaller than the primary form and greatly reduced vigor due to the heavy persistent variegation, but a beautiful and striking plant.

'Slender Crookstem'. In a high percentage of its culms, within the first several feet (1 m) of growth, the culm curves back and forth, deviating an inch or more (2.5 cm) from center, but returning to center and the original direction of growth. Unlike in *Phyllostachys aureosulcata*,

Phyllostachys bambusoides 'Marliac'

Phyllostachys bambusoides 'Richard Haubrich'

Phyllostachys bambusoides 'Richard Haubrich', cream and apricot coloration in the leaves.

the deviations are not abrupt. The curves may be simple, involving only two or three internodes, or complex, involving many internodes.

'**Subvariegata**'. Culms are lighter in color than the principal form. The leaves are smaller, with light green stripes on a darker green background. The variegation is most pronounced in the spring, then fades and softens. Somewhat interesting, but other cultivars are far more striking.

'**White Crookstem**'. The culms develop a deposit of white powder that persists and in older culms virtually obscures their green color.

Phyllostachys bissetii

Height: 16–40 ft. (5–12 m)
Diameter: 2 in. (5 cm) max.
Light: full sun
Zone 5

Vigorous, establishes rapidly, and is a good choice for a hedge. It seldom achieves the maximum cited height and more typically grows to about 20 ft. (6 m). The culms as well as the foliage leaves are dark green, and the culm leaves are

Phyllostachys bissetii

Phyllostachys dulcis

also predominantly green, offering an attractive backdrop for other bamboos and other plants.

This species is exceptionally cold hardy, and its rhizomes are reputedly even more resistant to cold than those of *Phyllostachys aureosulcata* or *P. nuda*. After hard winters, it is among the best in the genus for retaining a fresh, unbattered look. The early season shoots can be harvested for the table.

'Dwarf'. A smaller form, less than 20 ft. (6 m) tall. May be more cold hardy than the primary form.

Phyllostachys dulcis
Sweetshoot bamboo

Height: 20–40 ft. (6–12 m)
Diameter: 2¾ in. (7 cm) max.
Light: full sun
Zone 6

Called sweetshoot bamboo because of its mild-tasting shoots. It establishes rapidly and quickly yields large shoots. As it grows, it bends more toward the sunlight than many *Phyllostachys* plants do. It is also less steadfastly upright than many of the genus, its culms twisting and arching somewhat as they wander their way vertically, rapidly tapering toward the tip. It is not the best bamboo for narrow areas. The culm wood is not particularly good, but the early season shoots are choice. It is attractive, but somewhat less stately than others of the genus.

Phyllostachys edulis
Moso

Height: 30–90 ft. (9–27 m)
Diameter: 7 in. (18 cm) max.
Light: full sun
Zone 6

Formerly known by the botanical name *Phyllostachys heterocycla* f. *pubescens*. The change to the less tongue-twisting *P. edulis* is a welcome relief. It is also commonly known by its Japanese name, moso.

Phyllostachys dulcis, new shoots.

Phyllostachys edulis, showing the culm leaf beginning to separate from a new culm.

Phyllostachys edulis is the world's largest hardy bamboo. Only a few tropical bamboos grow larger. A single day's growth of a new culm has been measured at 46³/₅ in. (117 cm). The moso forests of China and Japan are one of nature's great beauties. In China, *P. edulis* forests cover more than 7 million acres (2.8 million hectares). More than two thirds of China's immense bamboo acreage is forested with this species.

The leaves, among the smallest of all *Phyllostachys*, contrast with the massive, towering culms. Its pendulous tops, nodding with masses of tiny shimmering leaves, are said to resemble giant green ostrich plumes. The internodes are relatively short, particularly near the base. New culms have a matt finish and the velvety coat of fine hairs.

The culm wood is thick, but softer and less resistant to cracking than that of other timber bamboos, such as *Phyllostachys bambusoides* and *P. nigra* 'Henon'. Nevertheless, it is widely

Phyllostachys edulis, showing distinctive fine velvety hairs on the surface of a new culm.

used as timber and pulpwood, and in a broad variety of craftworks. When polished, the thick-walled culms take on a characteristic decorative luster.

More *Phyllostachys edulis* shoots are harvested for food than any other bamboo species. It initiates shoots from fall through spring. Shoots initiated in fall and winter remain underground. Called winter shoots, they are highly regarded for their quality and are harvested as part of the seasonal cuisine. Spring shoots are also harvested for food, but they have some bitterness and, though very good, are less highly esteemed.

Although *Phyllostachys edulis* is the world's largest temperate bamboo, it is also one of the most difficult in the genus to establish. New plantings are not prone to failure, but they are often slow to develop the size and dramatic beauty of their native environments.

This bamboo is perhaps more particular about its growing environment than any other *Phyllostachys*. It benefits from ample moisture, warmth, and manure. It is intolerant of alkaline soils, but develops chlorosis if the soil is too acidic. In Japan, it attains greater size in the warmer south. Toward the north, less of it is grown, and its culm size is progressively smaller.

Other temperate-climate timber bamboos, such as *Phyllostachys vivax*, *P. bambusoides*, and *P. nigra* 'Henon', establish much more rapidly and reliably than *P. edulis*, attaining a larger size in the first years of growth. Even in some regions in the plant's native China, the largest culms in a 12-year-old grove may only achieve a height of 20 ft. (6 m) and a diameter of 2 in. (5 cm).

Phyllostachys edulis is highly desirable for the collector and hobbyist, but it cannot be universally recommended for the landscape when rapid spread and attainment of height are essential. Yet, in situations where slower growth and a range of possible maximum heights is acceptable, this is a highly desirable bamboo for the landscape and well worth the wait. While its beauty can only be fully appreciated in a mature forest, among the towering culms and masses of tiny shimmering leaves, many of its distinctive

Phyllostachys edulis along a pathway at Hakone Gardens, Saratoga, California.

features can nevertheless be appreciated on a smaller scale in the landscape or garden.

'**Anderson**'. From a grove at Anderson, South Carolina. It is reportedly more cold hardy.

'**Bicolor**'. Yellow culms and a green sulcus.

'**Goldstripe**'. New leaves are prominently white striped, fading to green by fall. The culm exhibits varying green and gold striping patterns. New shoot and branch tips are pale pink to cream colored.

'**Heterocycla**' (tortoise shell bamboo). A unique and famous cultivar. The common name comes from the culms that resemble the pattern of a tortoise shell: the internodes are bulged on one side, but nearly nonexistent on the other

Phyllostachys edulis 'Goldstripe'

Phyllostachys edulis 'Heterocycla'

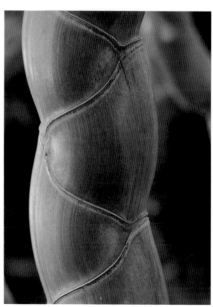

Phyllostachys edulis 'Heterocycla' showing its unique, bizarre, and highly ornamental culms, with unextended internodes on alternating sides.

side, never extending from the node. This pattern alternates from side to side along the length of the culm, creating an unusual and distinctive appearance. This cultivar is a highly valued ornamental in Japan and China, and its cured culms are also highly prized. It is an unstable form, and a plant may produce normal culms as well as the convoluted form. 'Heterocycla' occasionally arises spontaneously in natural stands of *Phyllostachys edulis*.

Phyllostachys flexuosa

Height: 18–32 ft. (5.5–9.6 m)
Diameter: 2¾ in. (7 cm) max.
Light: full sun
Zone 6

Phyllostachys flexuosa

A cold-hardy bamboo that tolerates difficult growing conditions, including wind and soils that are saline, sandy, or alkaline. The shoots initiate in early midseason and are considered choice. Some culms show pronounced zigzags. The foliage and branching are somewhat more open than average.

'**Kimmei**'. Yellow culms with a green sulcus. New foliage leaves are white tipped, gradually becoming more variegated with green.

'**Spring Beauty**'. New spring leaves are highly variegated. Culms are yellow, sometimes with a green sulcus, and turn reddish when new culms are exposed to the sun.

Phyllostachys glauca

Height: 20–40 ft. (6–12 m)
Diameter: 3 in. (7.5 cm) max.
Light: full sun
Zone 6

The young culms have an evenly distributed white waxy powder on their surface that gives them a very attractive, pronounced blue-green appearance. This look gradually dissipates throughout the growing season. Not stiffly erect, the culm tops are somewhat arching.

This species is reportedly tolerant of difficult growing conditions, such as poor or alkaline soils and some drought. In China, it grows on flood lands, plains, and hillsides. The good-tasting

Phyllostachys flexuosa 'Spring Beauty'

Phyllostachys glauca, displaying the distinctive coloration of new culms.

shoots are attractive, and they initiate in early midseason.

'Notso'. Similar to the primary form, but the new culms lack the waxy coating and blue-green coloration.

'Yunzhu'. Similar to the primary form, but with irregular, ornamental brownish purple spots on the culm. The new culms lack the waxy coating and blue-green coloration.

Phyllostachys heteroclada
Water bamboo

Height: 16–33 ft. (5–9.9 m)
Diameter: 1½ in. (4 cm) max.
Light: full sun
Zone 6

Vigorous and erect, this bamboo is a good choice for a screen or tall hedge. Mature culms are a dark gray-green. The rhizomes have air channels that enable *Phyllostachys heteroclada* to grow in wet and highly saturated soils, and the roots are also adapted to wet conditions, hence its name, water bamboo. It also grows well in normal soils.

Phyllostachys glauca 'Yunzhu'

'Purpurata'. Much smaller than the primary form. The slender culms have long internodes, a zigzag growth habit, and an arching profile. Wind, rain, and the weight of the foliage can readily bend the culms to the ground. The nodes are large with subhorizontal branches. The coloration of the culm leaf blade is distinctly purple throughout, rather than mostly green as in the other forms.

'Solidstem'. Slightly smaller than the primary form, the internodes on the lower half to two thirds of the culm are solid rather than hollow.

Phyllostachys humilis

Height: 12–20 ft. (4–6 m)
Diameter: 1 in. (2.5 cm) max.
Light: full sun
Zone 6

Phyllostachys heteroclada, tip of new shoot.

Phyllostachys heteroclada

One of the smallest species in the genus, *Phyllostachys humilis* is leafy and establishes rapidly. Excellent as a hedge plant, it takes well to vigorous pruning, or left relatively unpruned. Young culms are sometimes an attractive dark brown, turning green with maturity, or sometimes an orange-yellow in strong sun. This species is widely cultivated in Japan.

Phyllostachys iridescens

Height: 24–40 ft. (7.3–12 m)
Diameter: 2¾ in. (7 cm) max.
Light: full sun
Zone 6
Phyllostachys iridescens is native to China's Jiangsu and Zhejiang Provinces, and widely distributed elsewhere. It is a versatile bamboo, cultivated for its excellent tasting shoots, strong culm

Phyllostachys humilis

Phyllostachys iridescens, new shoots.

Phyllostachys kwangsiensis

wood, and an attractive specimen ornamental. The internodes often have indistinct yellowish striae running along their length, particularly near the base.

The cured culms are used for implement handles and construction. Because of the reddish culm leaf sheaths and the large, pendulous culm leaf blades reminiscent of a cock's comb, the new shoots are said to resemble red roosters in a bamboo grove.

Phyllostachys kwangsiensis
Height: 26–52 ft. (7.8–16 m)
Diameter: 4 in. (10 cm) max.
Light: full sun
Zone 7
Like moso, *Phyllostachys edulis*, new *P. kwangsiensis* culms have a dense pubescence. Introduce from China into Germany in the late 1980s, this species has been dubbed the

"moso of the north." It has demonstrated reasonable frost tolerance, but ironically it is native to the warmer southern Chinese province of Guangxi, and some Chinese literature describes it as tender. It is also cultivated in the Chinese provinces of Guangdong, Hunan, Jiangsu, and Zhejiang. The culm wood is hard and excellent for construction, furniture making, and weaving. The shoots are edible, but somewhat astringent.

Phyllostachys lithophila
Taiwan stone bamboo
Height: 16–40 ft. (5–12 m)
Diameter: 4¾ in. (12 cm) max.
Light: full sun
Zone 7
Phyllostachys lithophila is native to Taiwan and widely distributed throughout, though more intensely cultivated in central and northern parts.

Phyllostachys lithophila

The culms are strong and are used for construction and implements. The species is not commonly cultivated in the West.

Phyllostachys makinoi
Height: 24–60 ft. (7.3–18 m)
Diameter: 3 1/2 in. (9 cm) max.
Light: full sun
Zone 6

The new culms have a white powder on their surface, giving them a blue-green appearance. Like those of *Phyllostachys viridis*, the culms have minute dimples, which are noticeable by running a fingernail along the surface of the culm. *Phyllostachys makinoi* has a stiffly erect habit.

The culm wood is very hard and dense, and it is used in house construction, furniture manufacture, and pulpwood for paper. The midseason shoots are suitable for the table.

Although cold tolerant, this species needs a warm climate, ample water, fertilizer, and mulch to thrive and approximate its maximum height, growing less vigorously and smaller in cooler climates. It is one of the most widely cultivated bamboos in Taiwan.

Phyllostachys mannii
Height: 18–30 ft. (5.5–9 m)
Diameter: 2 1/2 in. (6.3 cm) max.
Light: full sun
Zone 6

Native to northern India, northern Burma, and southern China, this species is among the most tolerant of the genus with respect to drought, temperature extremes, high pH soils, and sandy soils. Shooting occurs in early to late midseason. Although the shoots are edible, they are rather astringent. The strikingly attractive culm leaves are dark purple to pale green or white striped with purple and green accents.

The culm leaf blade is unusually broad for a *Phyllostachys*. The culm wood is hard, durable, and resistant to cracking, and splits well for weaving. With exposure to sun, the light green culms may sometimes turn a yellow-orange.

'Decora'. From China's Yangtze Valley, this plant, once identified as a separate species, is now regarded as the same as *Phyllostachys mannii*, which was first identified in India. Mature 'Decora' specimens appear to be identical to the type species.

Phyllostachys meyeri
Height: 18–36 ft. (5.5–10.8 m)
Diameter: 2 1/4 in. (6 cm) max
Light: full sun
Zone 6

This species is very similar to *Phyllostachys aurea*, but it grows taller without the compressed lower internodes. Like *P. aurea*, it is also suited to hot climates as well as more temperate environments. It has an erect growth habit. The culm wood is strong and splits well. Midseason shoots are edible, though not choice.

Phyllostachys nidularia
Height: 18–33 ft. (5.5–9.9 m)
Diameter: 1 3/4 in. (4.4 cm) max.
Light: full sun
Zone 6

The culm nodes are very prominent and provide an attractive contrast to bamboos with less prominent nodes. The large culm leaf blades and exaggerated auricles have a distinctive appearance, and they are readily identifiable even while still tightly wrapped around the emerging shoot. Shoot initiation begins in early midseason.

The shoots are excellent and are free from bitterness even in the raw state. The culm wood is not strong, but is used for shrimp traps in China.

'Farcta'. The lower part of the culm is solid or nearly solid.

'June Barbara'. The leaves have a brushed variegated effect. The green in the leaf color is a light lime green, which may contribute to this attractive cultivar's unfortunate lack of vigor. It is less cold hardy and far smaller than the primary form.

'Smoothsheath'. This cultivar lacks the shaggy hairs on the sheath scars and the base of the culm leaf sheath.

Phyllostachys makinoi

Phyllostachys meyeri

Phyllostachys mannii 'Decora'. The showy culm leaf is more distinctive on mature specimens.

Phyllostachys nidularia, showing the distinctive, exaggerated auricles on the culm leaf embracing the new culm.

Phyllostachys nigra. The new culm in the foreground has not yet turned the deep, rich black characteristic of mature culms.

Phyllostachys nigra shoot.

Phyllostachys nigra
Black bamboo

Height: 20–55 ft. (6–17 m)
Diameter: 3¼ in. (8.3 cm) max.
Light: mostly sunny
Zone 6

Phyllostachys nigra is a beautiful, choice ornamental. The culms and branches are at first dark green, turning eventually to a deep solid black. The small green leaves contrast with the jet-black culms, branches, and branchlets.

This bamboo has long been highly valued as an ornamental in China and Japan, and is believed to be the first bamboo introduced into Europe, coming to England around 1827. It is widely cultivated in its native China, but is relatively rare in the wild. It is one of the more popular and desirable ornamentals in Asia and the West.

Phyllostachys nigra is often smaller in habit than its maximum size would suggest, particularly in warmer more southerly climates, where partial shading from hot afternoon sun is preferable. The plant prefers less intense sunlight and is less steadfastly upright than most species of the genus. It is also sensitive to salts in the water, sometimes showing tip burn on its leaves.

Its gracefully arching habit contributes to its considerable beauty, but also limits landscaping applications. It bends readily under the weight of rain or snow—or the weight of its own foliage, particularly on older culms that bear greater leaf mass.

Where a stiffly upright bamboo is required, it would not be the first choice. Although some might consider it a sacrilege, it can be topped and pruned to moderate its arching habit—or topped and pruned even more aggressively to make a highly attractive hedge.

The dried culms hold their color. The culm wood is thin, but hard, and is excellent for furniture and other craftwork. The late midseason shoots are edible though slightly astringent.

Growing conditions, as well as the presumed existence of various strains, may account for some of the size differences cited for the bamboo, as well as differences in the rate of

Phyllostachys nigra 'Hale'

Phyllostachys nigra 'Bory'

Phyllostachys nigra 'Megurochiku'

color change and color depth. Numerous cultivars are available. Some are clearly distinctive and unique. Others may be more a product of growing conditions, or of rather modest distinctions.

'Bory' (snakeskin bamboo, leopard-skin bamboo, tiger bamboo). 'Bory' is generally larger, more erect, and more heat tolerant than the primary form. The culm is spotted with brown to purplish black spots, sometimes described as a snakeskin or leopard-skin pattern. With exposure to strong sun, the culms are yellow-green with brown spots. On seasoned culms, the muted spotting pattern gives the culms a distinctive appearance that lends itself to decorative construction and craftwork. Shoot initiation occurs late in the season.

'Daikokuchiku'. This California variant is purportedly larger than the primary form and turns black more quickly.

'Hale'. Purportedly 'Hale' turns black more quickly and is smaller and more cold hardy than the primary form; however, the differences may simply be a matter of different growing conditions. In the U.S. Northeast, with its colder winters and hotter summers, 'Hale' is reportedly smaller and more cold tolerant than the principal form. In the Pacific Northwest, with the cooler summers and milder winters, it reportedly grows as large or larger than the principal form and does not turn black any more rapidly.

'Henon'. No doubt this is the true biological species, but because the distinctive black-culmed variant, *Phyllostachys nigra*, was described and named first, 'Henon', the true species, has been relegated to the status of a variety or cultivar. 'Henon' is a true timber bamboo with a potential maximum height of 65 ft. (20 m) and diameter of 5 in. (13 cm). It

Phyllostachys nigra 'Henon'

grows well in full sun. Unlike the primary form, 'Henon' culms and branches remain green and the growth habit is erect. It is a beautiful, large landscape bamboo, and it has excellent properties for commercial applications. Its culm walls are thicker than those of the primary form, but sustain the same profusion of delicate foliage. In Japan, it is distributed in colder, more mountainous regions than the other timber bamboos, *P. bambusoides* and *P. edulis*. Its late midseason shoots are somewhat astringent raw, but are good after parboiling.

'Megurochiku'. This form is generally similar to 'Henon', but the sulcus on older culms turns a dark purple-brown. At one time, 'Megurochiku' was a very rare bamboo, growing only on the Japanese island of Awaji, and was protected from collection. It has since made its way to bamboo nurseries, collectors, and growers, and is available from a number of sources.

'Mejiro'. Similar to 'Bory' but the sulcus has little or no brown coloration.

'Muchisasa'. The culms turn a brownish black rather than the full deep black of the primary form.

'Othello'. Reportedly smaller than the primary form with more tightly grouped culms that turn black more quickly.

'Punctata'. Black coloration is broken into irregular blotches. The degree of culm coloration may vary, sometimes eventually turning a more or less solid brownish black. Growing conditions or different strains may account for some of the variation. The reported distinctions are not always consistent.

'Shimadake'. Similar to 'Henon' but with occasional brown or blackish vertical stripes of varying widths along the length of the culm internodes.

'Tosaensis'. Similar to 'Bory' but with one or two elongated spots per internode.

Phyllostachys nuda

Height: 18–34 ft. (5.5–10.2 m)
Diameter: 1¾ in. (4.4 cm) max.
Light: full sun
Zone 5

Cold hardy but not tolerant of dry winter winds, *Phyllostachys nuda* grows in extensive forests in eastern China. It is thought to be among the most cold hardy of the genus, but some reports indicate that it may be somewhat less robust. It is, nonetheless, an excellent small-leaved ornamental suitable for hedges and medium to tall screens, or a specimen grove.

Its new culms are very attractive, with gradations of dark purple-brown and olive tones, loosely covered with white powder. The thick culm wood is good quality and is often used for the legs of furniture. The early season shoots are fleshy and choice. The name "nuda" alludes to the absence of auricles and fimbriae on both the culm and foliage leaf sheaths.

'Localis'. The basal portion of the culm is spotted or densely blotched with brownish purple coloration. The spots or blotches begin appearing on new culms at 6 to 12 months.

Phyllostachys parvifolia

Height: 26–40 ft. (7.8–12 m)
Diameter: 3 in. (7.5 cm) max.
Light: full sun
Zone 6

This species is native to China's Anhui Province and commonly cultivated in Zhejiang Province. Its shoots are considered choice for eating. *Phyllostachys parvifolia* is not yet commonly cultivated in the West, but is nonetheless well regarded for stately erect culms in established groves and for small leaves on relatively short branches. It develops size quickly even in cooler climates.

Phyllostachys platyglossa

Height: 16–26 ft. (5–7.8 m)
Diameter: 1½ in. (4 cm) max.
Light: full sun
Zone 6

Phyllostachys platyglossa comes from China's Zhejiang and Jiangsu Provinces, where it is grown for its delicious shoots. Although the culms are suitable for fences and minor construction, the culm walls are thin and the wood is not

Phyllostachys nuda

Phyllostachys platyglossa

Phyllostachys parvifolia

Phyllostachys praecox 'Prevernalis'

Phyllostachys praecox 'Viridisulcata'

particularly strong. It is an attractive moderate-size specimen plant, but is less optimal for a hedge as the lower nodes are bare of branches.

Phyllostachys praecox
Height: 18–33 ft. (5.5–9.9 m)
Diameter: 2 in. (5 cm) max.
Light: full sun
Zone 7
Shoot initiation occurs very early in the season, and the shoots are considered exceptional. In Shanghai and Zhejiang Provinces, China, the new shoots are the main early season fresh vegetable. The internodes are short, and those near the base often have yellow-green striae running the length of the internode.

'Prevernalis'. The internodes are smaller in diameter toward the middle of their length.

'Viridisulcata'. The culm is yellow with a green sulcus, and green pinstripes randomly run the length of the internodes. New shoots sometimes have a red blush.

Phyllostachys propinqua
Height: 18–30 ft. (5.5–9 m)
Diameter: 2 in. (5 cm) max.
Light: full sun
Zone 6
Phyllostachys propinqua is cultivated for shoot production in China. Shoot initiation occurs in late midseason. The hard culm wood is used for tool handles and small construction, and the culms split well for weaving.

Originally introduced to the United States in 1928 by F. A. McClure, the species was subsequently reintroduced from Germany, where it has proven its winter hardiness. The true identity of the plants in cultivation in Europe and the United States has been in question over the years, but without definitive outcome. Regardless of its correct name, it is a plant of merit.

'Beijing'. Larger leaves, faster growing, and hardier than the primary form, perhaps further calling into question the true identity of the plants in the garden trade.

Phyllostachys propinqua 'Beijing'

Phyllostachys rubromarginata
Height: 30–60 ft. (9–18 m)
Diameter: 3¹/₄ in. (8.3 cm) max.
Light: full sun
Zone 6

Long, slender internodes create more space between branches, so the foliage is less dense than in many other *Phyllostachys* species. The nodes are not prominent, and the culm diameter is generally smaller for a given height. These features give it a graceful if less "massive" look.

The upper culm leaf sheath margins are red. One of the Chinese names for the plant is "red-margined sheath bamboo," thus giving rise to its botanical name, *Phyllostachys rubromarginata*. It is reportedly tolerant of alkaline soils and strong winds, inhabiting scrubland and gullies in its native China. Some of the world's largest examples of this species grow in the U.S. Southeast, where it achieves a size significantly exceeding that cited in Chinese literature.

Phyllostachys rubromarginata, showing the red margins of the culm leaf from which its name is derived.

The culm wood is tough and splits well. Shooting begins late in the season. The shoots have only slight bitterness prior to parboiling and are considered good quality for eating.

It was the most vigorous and most productive of the bamboos studied in extensive tests in Alabama, producing the largest tonnage of dry wood per acre, far exceeding the yield of loblolly pine (*Pinus taeda*). It is an excellent candidate for paper pulp production. One of the more versatile bamboos, *Phyllostachys rubromarginata* is an excellent choice for landscape use, shoots, culm wood, and paper pulp.

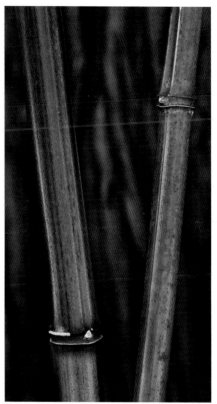

Phyllostachys stimulosa

Phyllostachys violascens

Phyllostachys stimulosa
Height: 16–26 ft. (5–7.8 m)
Diameter: 1½ in. (4 cm) max.
Light: full sun
Zone 6
Native to China's Zhejiang and Anhui Provinces, this hardy, smaller *Phyllostachys* species establishes quickly. New culms have a waxy coating of white powder. The culm nodes are prominent, and the culms do not split well. This species is useful in the landscape where a smaller member of the genus is required.

Phyllostachys violascens
Height: 20–50 ft. (6–15 m)
Diameter: 3 in. (7.5 cm) max.
Light: full sun
Zone 6

At its best, *Phyllostachys violascens* is a striking ornamental. The culms display a varied array of striping patterns and colors as they age. New culms have olive-green to purple-brown coloration and streaking, which is variously predominant or secondary to the green coloration.

As the culms age, the narrow, longitudinal color stripes become more distinct. The green and purple-brown colorations change to lighter green, yellow, straw yellow, and brownish crimson in varying degrees.

The degree of striping and coloration varies from culm to culm. Some descriptions appear to be at odds with other descriptions, suggesting that the new culms are a deep blackish violet, changing to yellow-green or yellow with age.

Some authorities have suggested that two or more species or forms are being described as the same taxon. The highly variable and progressively changing coloration of the culms, particularly when observed at different stages, may account for the variations.

New shoots appear early in the season. A third center branchlet at the node occurs more frequently than it does in most species of the genus.

The culm wood is not strong, but in China it is grown for its early spring shoots. In some climates it may run aggressively yet be slow to gain in stature.

Phyllostachys viridis

Height: 28–55 ft. (8.5–17 m)
Diameter: 3¾ in. (9.5 cm) max.
Light: full sun
Zone 6

A large timber bamboo with excellent tasting shoots, *Phyllostachys viridis* is one of the latest-shooting species of the genus. Its stance is sinuous rather than rigidly erect. Minute dimples on the surface of the culm are visible with a hand lens, and they can be felt by running a fingernail along the surface. The culm wood is hard and strong and can be readily split for weaving.

The species spreads slowly when grown in areas with relatively cool summers, such as the U.S. Pacific Northwest, though it still sizes-up fairly quickly. It performs even better in climates with warmer summers.

'Houzeau'. Green culms with a yellow sulcus.

'Robert Young'. Most *Phyllostachys* with multicolored culms carry the accent color in the sulcus of the internode. 'Robert Young' is among those with accent striping outside of the sulcus, along the ungrooved portion of the culm. The irregular green striping first appears as a darker color of green on the lighter, sulfur green culm. After a time, the culm changes to sulfur yellow and then to old gold, but the striping remains dark green. An occasional leaf blade shows cream-colored stripes. A highly desirable ornamental, 'Robert Young' also has the excellent shoot and culm-wood properties of the primary form. Propagules of *P. viridis* sometimes spontaneously generate new instances of 'Robert Young'.

Phyllostachys viridis 'Houzeau'

Phyllostachys viridis 'Robert Young'

Phyllostachys vivax

Phyllostachys vivax

Height: 35–70 ft. (10.5–21 m)
Diameter: 5 in. (13 cm) max.
Light: full sun
Zone 6

This choice, hardy, ornamental timber bamboo establishes and grows very rapidly. The species name alludes to the plant's vigorous growth. It is the most cold hardy of the large timber bamboos, and shoots in early midseason.

Phyllostachys vivax somewhat resembles P. bambusoides, but P. vivax culm walls are much thinner, the wood is inferior, and the culms are less straight. On the plus side, P. vivax establishes and attains a large size far more quickly than P. bambusoides, and its shoots are excellent for eating and free of bitterness even when raw.

For a Phyllostachys, it has large, broad leaves, giving it a bit of a tropical look. In the landscape, it is complemented by nearby smaller-leaved bamboos. For shoot production, or as a hardy,

Phyllostachys vivax 'Huangwenzhu'

Phyllostachys vivax shoot

Phyllostachys vivax 'Aureocaulis', culms with random green striping.

Phyllostachys vivax 'Aureocaulis'

Phyllostachys vivax 'Huangwenzhu Inversa'

ornamental timber bamboo, *P. vivax* is an outstanding selection.

Heavy rains and wind can fracture new culms of this lushly foliaged bamboo. Fracture is a greater risk if the adverse conditions occur just after the new culms have fully leafed out, but before the culms have sufficiently hardened. This can be more of a concern in newly developing groves where mature culms are not available for support. If this is a problem, the new culms can be topped slightly to reduce the burden.

'Aureocaulis'. Yellow culms with random green stripes and occasionally larger portions of green. Highly attractive, this and the other cultivars retain the vigor of the primary form. Randomly and spontaneously during propagation or in the ground, some of the *Phyllostachys vivax* cultivars may migrate to another of the cultivar forms.

'Huangwenzhu'. Green culms with a yellow sulcus.

'Huangwenzhu Inversa'. Yellow culms with a green sulcus.

PLEIOBLASTUS

Pleioblastus includes hardy dwarf, shrub, and even small arborescent bamboos with leptomorph rhizomes and a running habit. The generic name refers to the many branch buds. Each node bears from three to seven principal branches.

Largely of Japanese origin, *Pleioblastus* species are widely distributed in Japan and China. The genus encompasses a wide variety of variegated species and forms, providing the landscaper with a broad palette of colors and textures.

The leaves, which are arrayed near the tips of the culms and branches, are generally smaller and more slender than those of other shrub bamboos, such as *Sasa*, *Sasaella*, and *Indocalamus*. Although many *Pleioblastus* bamboos can be grown to the size of substantial shrubs, and some have an arborescent habit, the genus has become virtually synonymous with dwarf or groundcover bamboos.

For most groundcover or shrubby species of *Pleioblastus*, the slender culms and branches are overshadowed by proportionately larger leaves. Thus, the persistent or late-shedding culm leaves are generally not conspicuous. Nonetheless, the persistent culm leaves can give some of the more arborescent species a bit of a scruffy appearance.

If grown as a groundcover, *Pleioblastus* species benefit from an annual winter clipping, keeping their height in check and fostering spring growth of fresh-looking new culms, branches, and leaves. Because foliage of these species is often clipped or removed in the spring, winter leaf damage is less of an issue than with other bamboos. If winter scruffiness can be tolerated prior to spring renewal of the foliage, these bamboos can be grown in colder zones than cited, as long as the roots and rhizomes are protected and remain viable for the spring renewal.

Pleioblastus akebono

Pleioblastus akebono

Height: ½–2 ft. (15–60 cm)
Diameter: ¼ in. (0.6 cm) max.
Light: mostly shade
Zone 7
This highly attractive dwarf bamboo has leaves that are sometimes nearly all white when they emerge in the spring, turning greener as the season progresses. The green coloration looks as if it had been finely brushed on the white leaves, greener toward the leaf stem, whiter to all white toward the leaf tip. This bamboo grows very slowly and prefers shade and humidity.

Pleioblastus amarus

Height: 8–16 ft. (2.4–5 m)
Diameter: ¾ in. (2 cm) max.
Light: partial shade
Zone 6
The nodes may bear up to seven principal branches. The species is widely distributed in the Chang River Valley of China, where it is used for umbrella handles, flag poles, and similar items. The shoots are extremely bitter and are not harvested for food.

Pleioblastus amarus

Pleioblastus argenteostriatus

Pleioblastus argenteostriatus

Height: 1–3 ft. (30–90 cm)
Diameter: ¼ in. (0.6 cm) max.
Light: mostly shade
Zone 7

This variegated dwarf bamboo has varying amounts of creamy yellow striping in the leaves. Although it performs best with more shade, it is reasonably tolerant of sun. It is an attractive bamboo that can be enhanced by clipping or mowing in early spring to refresh its foliage.

Pleioblastus chino

Height: 2–12 ft. (0.6–4 m)
Diameter: ¾ in. (2 cm) max.
Light: mostly sunny
Zone 7

In the landscape, *Pleioblastus chino* and its various forms are often treated as groundcover or small shrub bamboos, but they can grow larger, into tall shrubs or hedges. The primary, non-variegated form is tolerant of full sun. The species and its forms are vigorous and have relatively

Pleioblastus chino

Pleioblastus chino 'Vaginatus Variegatus' grown as a tall shrub.

Pleioblastus chino 'Murakamianus'

deep running rhizomes. If allowed to grow larger, *P. chino* can spread aggressively.

'Angustifolia'. Very narrow leaves with modest white-striped variegation.

'Elegantissimus'. Leaves with very fine, white, often discontinuous stripes.

'Kimmei'. Leaves have several yellow-white stripes, and the culms are yellow with light green stripes.

'Murakamianus'. White-striped leaves are strongly but variably variegated. On average, three quarters of the leaf is white, but it may vary from all white to nearly all green. This cultivar is reasonably tolerant of sun, but prefers filtered light.

'Vaginatus Variegatus'. Smaller, narrower leaves than the primary form. Its delicate white striping is stronger than that of 'Elegantissimus', but not nearly as bold as 'Murakamianus'. Although generally grown as a groundcover, it

Pleioblastus chino 'Kimmei'

can be grown as a hedge or even as a specimen plant.

Pleioblastus distichus
Dwarf fernleaf
Height: 1/4–2 ft. (7.6–60 cm)
Diameter: 1/8 in. (0.3 cm) max.
Light: partial shade
Zone 6
One of the smallest bamboos, *Pleioblastus distichus* is an attractive, all-green groundcover with

Pleioblastus distichus

Pleioblastus gramineus

Pleioblastus fortunei

very small, tough, erect leaves. The leaf blades are arranged tightly in two ranks, resembling a fern. This arrangement is called distichus and is the source of the bamboo's botanical name.

Pleioblastus distichus can be used for bonsai, in a rock garden, as a groundcover, or even as a lawn, trimmed with a mower. It looks best when periodically clipped or mowed, fostering dense growth and a compact habit.

'Mini'. An even smaller version of the primary form.

Pleioblastus fortunei
Dwarf whitestripe
Height: 1–4 ft. (30–120 cm)
Diameter: 1/4 in. (0.6 cm) max.
Light: partial shade
Zone 7

A choice groundcover or shrub bamboo, Pleioblastus fortunei has crisply variegated, green and white, striped leaves. Unlike many variegated bamboos, it holds its variegation well through the summer's stronger sunlight, though more shaded conditions are preferable. One of the earliest bamboos to come to Europe, it was introduced into Belgium in 1863.

Pleioblastus gramineus
Height: 6–12 ft. (1.8–4 m)
Diameter: 1/2 in. (1.25 cm) max.
Light: mostly sunny
Zone 7

One of the taller, somewhat arborescent Pleioblastus species, this bamboo has slender grasslike leaves, giving it its species name. Attractive in spite of its persistent culm leaves, the plant has a fountainlike growth habit. It is native to the Ryukyu Islands of Japan and more tolerant of salt air than many bamboos. Although thin walled, the culms make excellent garden stakes. This species is sometimes used for bonsai.

'Monstrispiralis'. This form is indigenous to remote southern islands in Japan's Kagoshima Prefecture. As with the primary form, new culms are formed along leptomorph rhizomes, and also by tillering off an existing culm. Many of the tillering culms grow in a pronounced spiral.

Pleioblastus hindsii

Pleioblastus hindsii
Height: 8–20 ft. (2.4–6 m)
Diameter: 1 1/4 in. (3.2 cm) max.
Light: mostly sunny
Zone 7

Native to southern China and introduced to Japan centuries ago, Pleioblastus hindsii is among the more arborescent species of the genius. Its leaves and culms are a deep olive green and the leaves are considerably thicker and more leathery than those of most other bamboos. New leaves are initially quite erect, particularly toward the top of the plant. Although its leaves are wider than those of *P. gramineus* and *P. linearis*, they are nonetheless very slender, with an unusually narrow and extended leaf tip. The culm leaves are persistent.

This bamboo is reportedly quite tolerant of salt air. In China and Japan, it is grown as an ornamental. In southern Japan, it grows up to 20 ft. (6 m) tall, and its excellent shoots are harvested as a delicacy. Because some shooting often occurs throughout the growing season, it is a source of fresh shoots when others are unavailable.

Identification of the species is somewhat muddled. In the United States and England, and probably elsewhere, other bamboos have long ago been erroneously introduced as *Pleioblastus hindsii*. The leaves of the misidentified plants are wider, thin, and pliable, rather than thick and leathery, and they do not have an extended narrow leaf tip.

Pleioblastus kongosanensis

Height: 1–6 ft. (30–180 cm)
Diameter: ³⁄₈ in. (1 cm) max.
Light: mostly sunny
Zone 7

A useful but slightly scruffy groundcover or shrub bamboo from Japan, *Pleioblastus kongosanensis* is more of interest for collectors, as other choices in the genus have a more pleasing appearance in the landscape.

'Akibensis'. Hairy culms. Indigenous to central and southern Japan.

'Aureostriatus'. The most desirable of the forms. Green leaves with occasional gold stripes.

Pleioblastus linearis

Height: 8–18 ft. (2.4–5.5 m)
Diameter: 1 in. (2.5 cm) max.
Light: full sun
Zone 8

Native to Japan's Ryukyu Islands, *Pleioblastus linearis* is one of the larger, somewhat arborescent species in the genus. Its leaves are long, very slender, and grasslike, and its branches are densely ramified with abundant leaves, giving the plant a plumed appearance. It is reportedly tolerant of salt air.

The culms are used in fences and for making fish traps. In Okinawa, the culms with attached branches and leaves are traditionally used for roofing.

'Nana'. Smaller with narrower leaves.

Pleioblastus pygmaeus

Height: ¹⁄₂–2 ft. (15–60 cm)
Diameter: ¹⁄₈ in. (0.3 cm) max.
Light: partial shade
Zone 7

Pleioblastus kongosanensis 'Aureostriatus'

Pleioblastus linearis

Pleioblastus pygmaeus

Pleioblastus pygmaeus is a small, green, dwarf bamboo. Its exact origins and nature are somewhat vague. Plants from various sources demonstrate different characteristics, and *P. pygmaeus* may actually include several related species or forms. There has been no documented record of its flowering, thus making classification by traditional methods more difficult.

It is a common groundcover in the nursery trade, and may be found under a variety of names, such as "*Arundinaria pygmaea*," "*Bambusa pygmaea*," and "*Sasa pygmaea*." Some forms are more desirable than others, but in general, it is an attractive, if not spectacular, utilitarian groundcover. It can be mowed or clipped to a few inches tall, or allowed to grow taller depending on the landscaping need.

'Ramosissimus'. Grows taller and is more hardy than the primary form.

Pleioblastus shibuyanus 'Tsuboi'
Height: 2–9 ft. (0.6–2.7 m)
Diameter: ⅜ in. (1 cm) max.
Light: partial shade
Zone 6
This distinctive, variegated bamboo has relatively small leaves that create an interesting effect as

Pleioblastus shibuyanus 'Tsuboi'

the white striping blends into the green. A choice ornamental, it can be grown as a groundcover, shrub, hedge, small specimen plant, or container plant. The rhizome system is fairly robust and aggressive, particularly on larger plants.

Pleioblastus simonii
Medake
Height: 8–20 ft. (2.4–6 m)
Diameter: 1 ½ in. (4 cm) max.
Light: mostly sunny
Zone 7

Native to China and Japan, *Pleioblastus simonii* is one of the larger arborescent species of the genus and is reportedly very tolerant of salt air. It is commonly planted as an ornamental in China.

With its straight culms and erect habit, it is often used as a hedge bamboo, but its persistent and prominent culm and branch leaves give it a bit of a tattered look. The straight culms are thin walled but strong, without prominent nodes, and are ideal for garden stakes. In China, the culms are used to make fishing rods and cages.

The shoots are reportedly edible, but somewhat bitter. In many climates, shooting does not occur until mid to late summer, providing little time for the shooting and branching to be completed before the onset of winter's cold. For its size, it is not an aggressive runner.

'Variegatus'. The leaf shape and coloration vary considerably on the same culm, from wide to narrow, and from all green to variegated with white striping. The new culm leaves are initially attractively variegated, but soon fade and look increasingly scruffy with the passage of time. The cultivar is more aggressive than the type form and is not as attractive as other variegated bamboos.

Pleioblastus simonii

Pleioblastus simonii 'Variegatus'

Pleioblastus viridistriatus

Height: 1–6 ft. (30–180 cm)
Diameter: ³⁄₈ in. (1 cm) max.
Light: mostly shade
Zone 7

Pleioblastus viridistriatus is a striking ornamental groundcover or shrub for shaded environments. The new leaves are vivid chartreuse with darker green stripes. As the season progresses, the coloration becomes less vivid and, when grown in the sun, the leaves are far less colorful, darkening to green with somewhat darker green striping. The leaves can look tattered after even relatively mild winters.

In late winter or early spring, this bamboo should be clipped or mowed to remove most of the older leaves and make way for the showy new foliage. It does well in climate zones colder than zone 7, as long as the roots and rhizomes are protected and it is given a spring clipping.

Leaf size varies, but can range up to 8 in. (20 cm) long and 1¹⁄₂ in. (4 cm) wide on larger plants. Although it can reach a height of 6 ft. (1.8 m) in sunny conditions, it loses much of its appeal. It is at its excellent best in more shady conditions as a groundcover or small shrub.

'**Chrysophyllus**'. Similar to the type form, except the leaves are uniformly chartreuse with no striping.

PSEUDOSASA

Pseudosasa is a genus of mostly medium-sized to tall shrublike Asian bamboos with a solitary (or sometimes up to three in some species) principal branch at each node, leptomorph rhizomes, and a running habit. The genus is composed of some three dozen species.

Some of the largest species are arborescent. At the other end of the spectrum, *Pseudosasa owatarii* is a small shrub at its largest, and it is

Pleioblastus viridistriatus

more often encountered as a groundcover bamboo less than 1 ft. (30 cm) tall.

Pseudosasa culm leaves are leathery and persistent, or very late shedding. The foliage leaf blades are palmately arranged toward the top of the culms and tips of the branches.

Pseudosasa amabilis
Tonkin cane, tea stick bamboo

Height: 25–50 ft. (7.6–15 m)
Diameter: 2½ in. (6.3 cm) max.
Light: full sun
Zone 8

The famous Tonkin cane bamboo is highly regarded for its outstanding mechanical properties. It is still widely known by its earlier and longstanding botanical name, *Arundinaria amabilis*. The culms are strong, stiff, and resilient, with only a slight taper. The nodes are not prominent. In a mature stand, the culms are free of branches for one half to two thirds of their height.

When grown and processed properly, the top-graded, cured culms are entirely free of branch scars. Traditional uses for the species include poles for supporting hop plants, rug poles, fences, and handicraft. It is the only bamboo used for making the finest split-cane fly fishing rods.

Growing the bamboo to reach its famed potential is not easy, requiring a very warm temperate or cool semi-tropical environment. It does not propagate well from rhizome cuttings and can be very slow to establish.

If conditions are not ideal, the plants may not produce the highest quality culms that have made the species so notable. Introductions can be successful, however, since it is virtually unknown in natural stands, and the cultivated stands in southeastern China are the source of its reputation.

Pleioblastus viridistriatus 'Chrysophyllus'

Pseudosasa amabilis

Pseudosasa cantori

Height: 10–16 ft. (3–5 m)
Diameter: 1⅛ in. (3 cm) max.
Light: partial shade
Zone 7

Native to China's southern coastal provinces of Guangdong and Fujian, *Pseudosasa cantori* inhabits partially shaded, broad-leaved woodlands at elevations below 1600 ft. (500 m). The culm wood is used in making furniture.

Pseudosasa japonica

Arrow bamboo, yadake

Height: 10–18 ft. (3–5.5 m)
Diameter: ¾ in. (2 cm) max.
Light: mostly sunny
Zone 7

Pseudosasa japonica is one of the more widely cultivated bamboos in Europe, North America, and Asia. Introduced to Europe in 1850, it made its way to the United States by 1860, one of the earliest species introduced to America.

Each node generally has no more than a single principal branch. The culms are erect, and the ascendant branches bear drooping leaves up to 1 ft. (30 cm) long and 2 in. (5 cm) wide.

Reportedly tolerant of wind and salt air, it is a cold-hardy bamboo that grows as far north as the Japanese island of Hokkaido. A hedge 300 ft. (90 m) long was planted at the Rosewarne Experimental Horticultural Station in Cornwall, England, as a barrier against the strong Cornish

Pseudosasa cantori

Pseudosasa japonica 'Akebonosuji'

Pseudosasa japonica, with a groundcover bamboo.

Pseudosasa japonica 'Akebono'

Pseudosasa longiligula

gales. In a controlled trial of 400 species of hedging plants for sheltering purposes, *Pseudosasa japonica* was one of eight selected as most suitable.

Because the culm and branch leaves are persistent, and the branches ramify each year, mature, unkempt stands of *Pseudosasa japonica* can look scruffy and unattractive, but when well maintained, the upright culms and lush foliage are attractive and distinctive. It has the largest leaves of any widely available, semi-arborescent, hardy bamboo.

In the landscape, it is effective as a tall hedge, as a specimen plant, where it makes an elegant tall fountain, or as a container plant. To maintain a planting's appearance, older culms should be removed from the grove or clump.

During culm harvesting, the branches can be removed cleanly and easily by simply pulling them downward. The round, slender culms are thin walled, but relatively strong, with long internodes. The nodes are uninflated and have no groove or flattening above them. Because of

all these characteristics, the culms are suitable for making arrows, hence its common name—arrow bamboo. The culms also make excellent garden stakes.

'Akebono'. The leaves have white variegation that is predominant toward the tip. Some leaves may be nearly all white, others nearly all green. The plant may not reliably maintain its variegation, and culms with mostly green leaves may need to be removed to maintain the variegated look.

'Akebonosuji'. The leaves are variegated with creamy yellow stripes and may also display variegation similar to 'Akebono'. The leaf coloration in 'Akebonosuji' is somewhat more stable than 'Akebono', but reversion to mostly all green leaves is not uncommon.

'Pleioblastoides'. Rapidly developing secondary branches.

'Tsutsumiana'. The internodes are swollen near their base, resembling a green onion. This plant requires some effort to display its ornamental features, including thinning away less charac-

Pseudosasa owatarii

Pseudosasa usawai

teristic culms and removing the culm leaves to expose the swollen internodes.

'Variegata'. Similar to, if not the same as, 'Akebonosuji'.

Pseudosasa longiligula
Height: 14–26 ft. (4.3–7.8 m)
Diameter: 2 in. (5 cm) max.
Light: partial shade
Zone 7
From the northern Guangxi Province in southern China, this species is one of the taller and more robust of the genus. The thick, strong culms, long internodes, and even nodes are excellent properties for making furniture and smaller-scale items. The new shoots are excellent for the table.

Pseudosasa owatarii
Height: ¹/₂–3 ft. (15–90 cm)
Diameter: ¹/₄ in. (0.6 cm) max.
Light: partial shade
Zone 7

This attractive, small-leaved, dwarf species often grows only a few inches high. An excellent specimen for bonsai, it is endemic to the southern Japanese island of Yakushima.

Pleioblastus pygmaeus is sometimes confused with *P. owatarii*, but *P. owatarii* has shinier, more tapering leaves, in more of a palmate arrangement, rather than the fernlike arrangement of *P. pygmaeus* leaves.

Pseudosasa usawai
Height: 8–16 ft. (2.4–5 m)
Diameter: ³/₄ in. (2 cm) max.
Light: partial shade
Zone 7
Native to Taiwan and widely distributed throughout the island, *Pseudosasa usawai* grows in thickets in forests and open grasslands at elevations up to about 4000 ft. (1200 m). Exaggerated long brown hairs on the culm leaf margins add interest. It is somewhat less cold hardy than the other zone 7 pseudosasas.

Pseudosasa viridula

Raddia distichophylla

Pseudosasa viridula

Height: 10–18 ft. (3–5.5 m)
Diameter: ¾ in. (2 cm) max.
Light: partial shade
Zone 7
This species is native to Zhejiang Province in eastern China. The leaves are long and wide. Landscaping uses are similar to the more common *Pseudosasa japonica*. Culm leaves are persistent.

RADDIA

Raddia species are attractive, tropical, herbaceous bamboos that exhibit nocturnal "sleep" movements, with leaf blades that fold upward along the culm at night. This curious phenomenon typically begins at sunset and progresses over a four-hour period, reversing itself at dawn. The sleep movements also occur when a plant is under moisture or temperature stress.

Members of the genus inhabit low-altitude forest understories in Brazil and countries to the north. They can be found growing in sandy soil alongside cacti, or in scrub forest with bromeliads.

Some of the species have an attractive, fern-like leaf pattern. Bamboo gardeners and collectors tend to regard herbaceous bamboos as a relatively recent phenomenon in cultivation, but *Raddia* has been cultivated in France, as a greenhouse plant, for nearly a century and a half.

Raddia distichophylla

Height: 4–12 in. (10–30 cm) estimated
Diameter: 1/8 in. (0.3 cm) max.
Light: partial shade
Zone 10

Among the most attractive of the herbaceous bamboos, *Raddia distichophylla* has multiple pairs of deep green leaves that give it a delicate fernlike appearance. And, adding to the drama, as with all of the genus, the leaves fold upward at night. This species is currently very rare in cultivation.

RHIPIDOCLADUM

Rhipidocladum species are New World bamboos with pachymorph rhizome systems and a tight clumping habit. The thin-walled, weak culms begin erect, then arch and droop, or they climb or clamber on nearby supports. The culm leaves have a distinctly triangular profile.

The plants prefer humid growing conditions. Native habitats range from sea level to 9500 ft. (2900 m), from northwestern Argentina and central Brazil to northeastern Mexico.

The genus name refers to the characteristic fanlike branching pattern. There are approximately 23 known species, 17 of which have been described and classified.

Rhipidocladum racemiflorum

Height: 10–35 ft. (3–10.5 m)
Diameter: 1 in. (2.5 cm) max.
Light: mostly sunny
Zone 10

This clambering bamboo depends on trees to support its slender culms, manifold branches, and tufts of small leaves. It is one of the most widespread species in the genus. Where growing conditions are amenable, it makes a delicate and highly attractive ornamental.

SASA

A genus of cold-hardy, robust, shrublike bamboos, *Sasa* has a leptomorph rhizome and a running habit that is often aggressive. There is a single branch per node, which typically approxi-

Rhipidocladum racemiflorum

mates the diameter of the culm itself. The leathery culm and branch leaves are usually persistent. Foliage leaves are generally broad and large.

Sasa species are endemic to Asia, primarily Japan for the majority of the species, though Korea and China are also native ground. They densely cover large expanses of grasslands or forest understory in northern Japan. Most sasas prefer shade.

Although *Sasa* is distributed as far south as Hainan Island in the South China Sea, the genus is primarily associated with northern climates. It is the northernmost naturally distributed bamboo genus, extending to latitude 50°N on Sakhalin Island. The genus is distributed from sea level to approximately 8900 ft. (2700 m).

Historically, *Sasa* has been used as a catchall term to signify small shrublike, rather than

Sasa species

A large-leafed *Sasa* bamboo accents a bamboo fence line.

arborescent, bamboos. The Japanese word *sasa* is thought to derive from the Chinese *hsai-chu*, meaning small bamboo.

Although many sasas are attractive plants, nearly all species suffer from some withering of the leaf tips or margins. One ornamental species, *Sasa veitchii*, has strongly withered leaf margins, giving the plant a desirable, variegated look. In the plant's native environments, the weight of winter snow bends the flexible culms to the ground, covering the leaves and buds, and protecting them from cold winds and desiccation. With the spring snowmelt, the culms become upright, and the evergreen leaves begin to photosynthesize again.

Sasa hayatae

Height: 1–4 ft. (30–120 cm)
Diameter: ¼ in. (0.6 cm) max.
Light: mostly shade
Zone 5

Sasa hayatae comes from central and southern Japan. It resembles the more widely known *S. veitchii*, with leaves that wither at the margins as winter approaches, giving the appearance of

beige-white variegation around the margins of the green leaves. It is shorter and has smaller leaves than *S. veitchii*. This plant was previously misidentified in the garden trade as *S. veitchii* 'Minor'.

Sasa kurilensis

Height: 3–10 ft. (0.9–3 m)
Diameter: ¾ in. (2 cm) max.
Light: mostly shade
Zone 6

Sasa kurilensis is one of Japan's most prevalent bamboos. The specific name is derived from one of its native habitats, the Kuril Islands, a group of Russian islands northeast of Japan. Also distributed in northeastern Korea and Russia, the species extends as far as 50°N, to Russia's Sakhalin Island, where it thrives in a cold, wet, snowy environment. Its leaves are up to 10 in. (25 cm) long and 3 in. (7.5 cm) wide.

The new shoots are popular in northeastern and central Japan. Although seldom grown commercially, they are gathered in the wild, and licenses are sometimes issued to protect against overharvesting. The shoots are relatively small in

Sasa hayatae

Sasa kurilensis 'Simofuri'

diameter, but usable shoots are commonly harvested at a length of 8 in. (20 cm), and they are often salt pickled in the manner of other Japanese vegetables.

'Simofuri'. A distinctive and highly attractive ornamental. The leaves are up to 10 in. (25 cm) long and 2 in. (5 cm) wide, and are variegated with fine white stripes, giving the appearance that the variegation was applied with a brush stroke. The new shoots are also an attractive feature, particularly on larger plants, with soft yellow culms setting off culm leaves with red margins. This bamboo needs partial shade to look its best, and it is not well suited to hot, dry environments.

Sasa nagimontana

Height: 1–2 ft. (30–60 cm)
Diameter: 1/8 in. (0.3 cm) max.
Light: mostly shade
Zone 6
This species comes from Mount Nagi in Japan. Most sasas are large shrubs, but *Sasa nagimontana* fulfils a landscaping need for a dwarf large-leaved bamboo.

Sasa nagimontana

Sasa kurilensis

Sasa oshidensis

Height: 3–6 ft. (90–180 cm)
Diameter: ¼ in. (0.6 cm) max.
Light: partial shade
Zone 5

This vigorously growing shrub bamboo has large wavy leaves. It shows greater tolerance for heat and sun than many others of the genus and also looks attractive after a hard winter when others show leaf burning.

Sasa oshidensis

Sasa palmata

Height: 5–10 ft. (1.5–3 m)
Diameter: ½ in. (1.25 cm) max.
Light: mostly shade
Zone 7

Widely distributed in the Western world, *Sasa palmata* was introduced into England in 1889 and the United States in 1925. Potentially very invasive, the species covers vast areas of land in mountainous regions of its native Japan, growing in the wild from the country's southernmost areas to its northernmost islands. It is also found on the Korean island of Cheju-do in the south, and Russia's Sakhalin Island in the north.

It is one of the largest-leaved bamboos of the genus, with leaves up to 15 in. (38 cm) long and 3½ in. (9 cm) wide. Although *Sasa palmata* is very cold hardy, its thick, pea green, leathery leaves give it a tropical appearance.

As with many sasa bamboos, the leaf tips and margins tend to show withering from winter cold. If one accepts that the foliage naturally shows burning following winter, *Sasa palmata* could readily be rated to a colder zone 6, as it is otherwise very hardy.

It is an aggressive runner, particularly in cool climates, where it grows tallest and is most vigorous. In warmer, sunny climates, it needs shade to look its best. It is an excellent container plant.

Sasa senanensis

Height: 3–7 ft. (0.9–2.1 m)
Diameter: ½ in. (1.25 cm) max.
Light: mostly shade
Zone 6

Sasa senanensis is widely distributed in the mountainous regions of Japan, reaching as high as the lower alpine zone. It is similar to *S. palmata*, but distinguished by the hairy undersides of its leaves.

Sasa palmata

Sasa senanensis

172

Sasa tsuboiana

Sasa tsuboiana
Height: 3–6 ft. (90–180 cm)
Diameter: 1/4 in. (0.6 cm) max.
Light: mostly shade
Zone 6
Native to the central and southern regions of Japan, where it reaches elevations of up to 4100 ft. (1250 m), *Sasa tsuboiana* is among the most attractive of the sasas. Distinctively dark green, its glossy leaves are up to 11 in. (28 cm) long and 2 1/2 in. (6.3 cm) wide. It does not run as aggressively as *S. palmata*.

Sasa veitchii
Height: 2–5 ft. (60–150 cm)
Diameter: 1/4 in. (0.6 cm) max.
Light: mostly shade
Zone 6
An unusual ornamental bamboo, *Sasa veitchii* has attractive dark green leaves that wither at the margins as winter approaches, giving the appearance of having beige-white variegation rimming a dark green leaf. This species is somewhat smaller-leaved than many others of the genus,

Sasa veitchii

Sasaella masamuneana 'Albostriata'

though its leaves still measure up to 10 in. (25 cm) long and 2¼ in. (6 cm) wide.

When grown in a small container with only a few culms, the withered leaf margins may simply give the impression of an unhealthy plant. In a larger container, as a groundcover, or as a mounded shrub, however, the pseudo-variegation can be strikingly attractive, particularly in the winter months, when the landscape may be looking a bit dull. The best landscaping strategy may be cutting it to the ground in the spring, enjoying the fresh, new, green foliage through summer, and appreciating the green and beige variegated display in the winter.

Somewhat invasive, height and vigor can be reduced by cutting the plant to the ground after its initial flush of spring growth. Alternately, for more robust growth, cut the plant before spring growth begins.

SASAELLA

Sasaella is somewhat similar to *Sasa*, but the leaves are typically narrower for their length and smaller, and the culms have one to three branches per node. The rhizomes are leptomorph and the plants are rather aggressive runners.

In landscaping, because of their larger form, *Sasa* species are generally employed as shrubs, while *Sasaella* species serve as groundcovers as well as shrubs.

Endemic to Japan, *Sasaella* species are distributed from about latitude 31°N to 41°N, centered primarily on Honshu, the main central island of Japan. They are not distributed nearly as far north as *Sasa*.

Sasaella masamuneana
Height: 1½–6 ft. (45–180 cm)
Diameter: ¼ in. (0.6 cm) max.
Light: partial shade
Zone 7
This bamboo has elongated medium-sized leaves. It spreads rapidly, particularly when allowed to grow taller. The variegated forms are far more popular and widely grown than the green-leaved form. Except for leaf burn, it is easily hardy to a colder zone 6; however, since the species, and particularly the variegated forms,

benefit from radical pruning in early spring to refresh the foliage, winter leaf burn may not be a particular issue.

Sasaella ramosa

Sasamorpha borealis

'Albostriata'. An attractive, vigorous, variegated dwarf bamboo. The first of the glossy leathery leaves to appear are strongly variegated with creamy white striping. Later leaves may be much less variegated. 'Albostriata' benefits from an early spring trimming to refresh its foliage and emphasize the bright variegation.

'Aureostriata'. Similar to 'Albostriata', but the variegation is golden yellow rather than creamy white.

Sasaella ramosa
Height: 1½–6 ft. (45–180 cm)
Diameter: ¼ in. (0.6 cm) max.
Light: mostly sunny
Zone 7

Typically much smaller than its stated maximum height, the green-leaved *Sasaella ramosa* is often no more than 1½ ft. (45 cm) tall. Given the right soil and climate, it is a highly aggressive and dominant runner, and must be planted with care. In the garden trade, it is one of the plants often erroneously labeled "*Sasa pygmaea.*"

SASAMORPHA
A small genus consisting of approximately six species, *Sasamorpha* includes bamboos with large leaves, leptomorph rhizomes, and a running habit. The plants are generally similar in appearance to *Sasa*, but differ in that *Sasamorpha* culms have a more erect habit and the nodes are not prominently swollen. *Sasamorpha* is distributed in Japan, Korea, and China, at a latitude range of 28°N to 44°N.

Sasamorpha borealis
Height: 3–6 ft. (90–180 cm)
Diameter: ¼ in. (0.6 cm) max.
Light: mostly shade
Zone 6

Sasamorpha borealis is widely distributed from Hokkaido, one of Japan's more northerly islands, through the southern island of Kyushu, and in Korea. New culms are relatively upright. Mature clumps can look somewhat tattered and unkempt.

SCHIZOSTACHYUM

An Old World tropical genus with a pachymorph rhizome system and a clumping habit, *Schizostachyum* is distributed from southern China through Southeast Asia and the Pacific Islands. Except for one known clambering species, these bamboos have culms with an erect growth habit with drooping tips.

The nodes bear many short branches. The thin-walled culms are light for their size and are used for rafts, roofing, water containers, musical instruments, and numerous other craft items.

Plants may continuously flower without danger of dying, but often few viable seed are produced. There are some 45 known species.

Schizostachyum brachycladum
Height: 20–50 ft. (6–15 m)
Diameter: 4 in. (10 cm) max.
Light: full sun
Zone 10

This species is distributed in southern China and the Asia-Pacific. The yellow-culmed forms are exceptional ornamentals. Some variants have solid yellow culms. Others have green-striped culms as well as leaves with yellow striping. The short branches do not emerge until mid-culm, forming a crown for the erect, tightly clumped culms. The culms of the green form are used as cooking vessels for rice. The culms are also used for musical instruments and other handicraft.

'Bali Kuning'. Yellow culms with sporadic thin green stripes. Leaves have occasional creamy white stripes.

SEMIARUNDINARIA

Native to Japan, though also growing in the wild in mainland China, Taiwan, and Korea, likely from long ago introductions from Japan, *Semiarundinaria* species are arborescent or shrublike with a leptomorph rhizome system and a running habit. After *Phyllostachys*, *Semiarundinaria* is the most common genus of medium-sized temperate bamboos.

Some botanists regard *Semiarundinaria* as a cross between *Phyllostachys* and *Pleioblastus*.

Though somewhat similar, *Semiarundinaria* and *Phyllostachys* can be readily distinguished. Culms of *Phyllostachys* have a pronounced sulcus running the full length of the internode on the branching side, while culms of *Semiarundinaria* are mostly round, with a partial sulcus or flattening of the internode, primarily just above the node.

Semiarundinaria culm leaves cling slightly longer than those of *Phyllostachys*, hanging from

Schizostachyum brachycladum, with flower clusters.

the middle of their base before dropping completely. *Phyllostachys* culm leaves hang briefly from the edge of their base, rather than the middle, before dropping.

The culm leaf sheaths of *Semiarundinaria* are harder and thicker than those of *Phyllostachys*. *Semiarundinaria* also has three principal branches, as compared to two in *Phyllostachys*. The foliage leaves of *Semiarundinaria* are gen-

Semiarundinaria fastuosa, with the culm leaf hanging by the center of the sheath base before falling away, characteristic of the genus.

erally broader and deeper green than those of *Phyllostachys*, offering a different textural effect in the landscape.

Semiarundinaria fastuosa

Height: 20–34 ft. (6–10.2 m)
Diameter: 1¾ in. (4 4 cm) max.
Light: full sun
Zone 6

Long a popular ornamental bamboo, this species is the tallest and stateliest of the genus. It is steadfastly erect and thus a good choice in narrower confines where arching culms would be intrusive. Native to Japan, it is distributed in Taiwan and mainland China and was introduced into Europe in the 1890s.

When exposed to sun, the green culms and branches gradually turn a brick red or purple-brown color. The culm internodes are slightly grooved just above the branches. The culms are not particularly strong, but the shoots are edible and distinctively flavored.

It is valued in the landscape as a specimen or tall hedge. A dense screen can be achieved in narrow confines by hedging back the branches. In subsequent years, the branches ramify and produce more foliage leaves, creating a dense erect screen requiring very little depth.

Under most conditions, it is not an aggressive runner, though its rhizomes typically grow deeper than a *Phyllostachys* of corresponding size. It is reportedly tolerant of high pH soils and salt air.

'Viridis'. The culms and branches are a vivid dark green and remain so even with sun exposure. Even with age, the culms retain their vivid dark green color better than a typical green-culmed phyllostachys.

Semiarundinaria fortis

Height: 14–26 ft. (4.3–7.8 m)
Diameter: 1½ in. (4 cm) max.
Light: full sun
Zone 6

Native to Japan, primarily north of the southern island of Kyushu, this species is somewhat similar to the much more widely cultivated

Semiarundinaria fortis

Semiarundinaria makinoi

tSemiarundinaria fastuosa*, but smaller in stature. Its dark green leaves and culms provide a contrasting backdrop to other bamboos.

Semiarundinaria makinoi
Height: 8–16 ft. (2.4–5 m)
Diameter: ¾ in. (2 cm) max.
Light: mostly sunny
Zone 6
Semiarundinaria makinoi is among the smaller species of the genus. The culms are initially green, turning reddish brown with age and exposure to sun.

Semiarundinaria okuboi
Height: 10–25 ft. (3–7.6 m)
Diameter: 1½ in. (4 cm) max.
Light: full sun
Zone 6
One of the few large-leaved temperate-climate bamboos that thrive in heat and strong sunlight, this species is also one of the few broad-leaved temperate bamboos that have a somewhat arborescent habit and the capability of achieving significant height, though it seldom approaches its cited maximum height.

Its role in the landscape is diminished only by the propensities of its rampantly spreading rhizome system. Numerous rhizomes run fast, long, and deep. A rhizome barrier that would be easily sufficient for a much larger *Phyllostachys* bamboo may not be adequate to contain *Semiarundinaria okuboi*, particularly if the soil is loose and loamy, or if the barrier depth is marginal. If its spread is effectively managed, it is an attractive plant for the landscape. It also makes an excellent container plant. Its broad leaves contrast nicely with smaller-leaved phyllostachys.

Semiarundinaria yamadorii (hort.)
Height: 8–25 ft. (2.4–7.6 m)
Diameter: 1¼ in. (3.2 cm) max.
Light: full sun
Zone 6
Smiarundinaria yamadorii is regarded as the same species as *S. yashadake*. The plants in cultivation, however, generally have a more arching habit than *S. yashadake* and culms that are less straight. *Semiarundinaria yamadorii* (hort.) is common in the bamboo garden trade in the United Kingdom, but uncommon in the United States.

'Brimscombe'. The plant has yellowish lime-green color tones. New leaves are light yellow with faint green striping, but the color distinctions dissipate as the season progresses.

Semiarundinaria yashadake
Height: 8–25 ft. (2.4–7.6 m)
Diameter: 1¼ in. (3.2 cm) max.
Light: full sun
Zone 6

Semiarundinaria yamadorii 'Brimscombe' (hort.)

Semiarundinaria okuboi

Semiarundinaria yashadake 'Kimmei'. The variegation on the culm leaves echoes that of the culms.

Once classified as a variety of *Semiarundinaria fastuosa*, *S. yashadake* has more slender culms and a less upright habit, fewer branches, and broader leaves. So far, the plants sold as *S. yashadake* in the garden trade have been considerably shorter than the indicated maximum height.

'Kimmei'. A very attractive ornamental, much more widely grown than the primary form. The culms are yellow with a vertical green stripe on the internode. The culms may take on pink and red tones when exposed to the sun. The dark green leaves have occasional cream-colored

Semiarundinaria yashadake

striping. The culms are smaller in diameter for their height than others of the genus and produced in greater numbers, giving the plant a more delicate willowy appearance.

SHIBATAEA

These shrublike bamboos have leptomorph rhizomes and a running habit, though they are not aggressive runners. The culm nodes have three to seven main branches, which do not further ramify. The branches are unusually short, typically with only one to two internodes. There are no secondary branches. Leaf-bearing nodes have one, or rarely two, leaves.

Shibataeas have a compact form, and in the landscape are excellent shrubs, low hedges, or tall groundcovers. The short branches give them a look not normally associated with bamboos.

The genus consists of approximately 10 species. They are endemic to eastern China, though one species, *Shibataea kumasaca*, grows in the wild in southern Japan.

Shibataea chinensis

Height: 1–5 ft. (30–150 cm)
Diameter: ⅛ in. (0.3 cm) max.
Light: partial shade
Zone 6
Native to mountain slopes in forests or forest margins of China's Zhejiang, Anhui, Jiangsu, and Jiangxi Provinces, *Shibataea chinensis* is cultivated in China as an ornamental hedge. It is similar to *S. kumasaca*, but is usually shorter and not as sensitive to alkaline soil conditions.

Shibataea kumasaca

Height: 2–7 ft. (60–210 cm)
Diameter: ¼ in. (0.6 cm) max.
Light: partial shade
Zone 6
Native to the mountain slopes of Fujian and Zhejiang Provinces, China, *Shibataea kumasaca* is cultivated in other parts of mainland China, Taiwan, and Japan. It is the most widely cultivated and popular species of the genus, introduced into Britain in 1861 and into the United States in 1902.

Shibataea chinensis

Shibataea kumasaca

Shibataea kumasaca. The characteristic short, broad leaves on short branches are unusual for a bamboo.

This attractive plant is rather unique in appearance for a bamboo, with its squat broad leaves on short branches and compact growth habit. It prefers acidic soil, and easily shows leaf burn if grown in alkaline or even only slightly acidic conditions.

The rhizomes are relatively shallow and moderately spreading, making control easier than many of the tall shrub bamboos. It is more tame in this regard than most species of *Pleioblastus*. In a clump, the leaves generally obscure the culms, and the plant is excellent material for trimming into hedges or mounds.

'Albostriata'. White-striped leaves. The plants now in cultivation originated from plants collected in Japan's Aichi Prefecture in 1967. It tends to revert to all green leaves. Culms with green leaves must be removed to sustain the plant's variegation.

'Aureostriata'. Yellow-striped leaves. Introduced into Germany from Japan as early as 1865. Like 'Albostriata', it tends to revert to all green leaves and must be managed in the same manner.

SINOBAMBUSA

Sinobambusa species are native to southern China, the islands of Hainan and Taiwan, and northern Vietnam. Naturalized introductions include Japan, India, and Hawaii.

Somewhat resembling *Semiarundinaria*, *Sinobambusa* bamboos are arborescent or tall and shrublike, with leptomorph rhizomes and a running habit. The culm internodes are long and slender and compressed or flattened for a distance above the node. Culm leaves are

Sinobambusa intermedia

Sinobambusa tootsik 'Albostriata'

promptly deciduous, leaving a prominent corky sheath scar at the node. The nodes usually have three, but occasionally five to seven, main branches.

In the field, *Sinobambusa* can be distinguished from *Semiarundinaria* by culm leaves that drop away promptly and completely, whereas those of *Semiarundinaria* cling for a time by the base of the sheath before dropping. As a group, *Sinobambusa* species are attractive bamboos, but they are less hardy than *Semiarundinaria* or *Phyllostachys*.

Sinobambusa intermedia

Height: 12–16 ft. (4–5 m)
Diameter: 1 in. (2.5 cm) max.
Light: mostly sunny
Zone 8
New culms have a strikingly intense white powdery coating. At mid-culm, the internodes are up to 24 in. (60 cm) long. The foliage leaves are up to 8 in. (20 cm) long and 1 in. (2.5 cm) wide. In many climates this bamboo grows well in a range of sunlight conditions from partial shade to full sun.

Sinobambusa tootsik
Chinese temple bamboo

Height: 16–40 ft. (5–12 m)
Diameter: 2¼ in. (6 cm) max.
Light: mostly sunny
Zone 8
Perhaps the most widely cultivated species of the genus, *Sinobambusa tootsik* is native to China and was introduced into Japan during the Tang Dynasty, more than a millennium ago. It is an

ornamental often planted around temples and monasteries.

The slender culms, long internodes, and many secondary branches bear attractive foliage leaves. Its form is slender and graceful, with tufts of foliage. In cool, shadier conditions, it spreads slowly, but it spreads extremely vigorously in warmer sunny climates and is among the few running temperate climate bamboos that also grow well in subtropical climates. It is intolerant of dry cold winters.

'Albostriata'. One of the few large arborescent bamboos with heavily variegated leaves. The leaves are vividly variegated with cream-colored stripes. It is somewhat smaller and less vigorously growing than the primary form.

THAMNOCALAMUS

Indigenous to the Himalayas and Africa, *Thamnocalamus* is a genus of relatively hardy bamboos with pachymorph rhizome systems and a clumping habit. Except for *T. tessellatus*, the species have a delicate appearance and generally resemble *Fargesia* species, though they are not as cold hardy as the hardiest of the *Fargesia*.

Five Himalayan species have been identified. They typically inhabit mixed coniferous forests at elevations of 9200 to 11,500 ft. (2800 to 3500 m). New shoots come in summer to fall. The Himalayan species, like most montane bamboos of that region, are intolerant of warm soils and high summer heat and humidity.

Thamnocalamus crassinodus

Height: 10–25 ft. (3–7.6 m)
Diameter: ³/₄ in. (2 cm) max.
Light: partial shade
Zone 8

Thamnocalamus crassinodus 'Aristatus', showing the upright culm leaf blade and swollen nodes.

Thamnocalamus crassinodus 'Mendocino'

Native to Nepal and Tibet, *Thamnocalamus crassinodus* is more delicate in appearance than most *Fargesia* species. The small leaves are even smaller on some variants. The nodes are slightly swollen and the culms are brittle, so it is not the first choice for weaving in its native habitat, but it provides fodder for livestock, shelter for birds, and food for the small red panda. A number of variants are found in different locales and have made their way into cultivation in the Western world.

'**Aristatus**'. Delicate smaller leaves and more strongly swollen culm nodes. New culms may turn red with exposure to sun.

'**Kew Beauty**'. Very small leaves. Culms turn red to dark brownish red with age.

'**Mendocino**'. Large blue-green leaves with a pronounced droop. Among the larger and faster growing of the forms.

'**Merlyn**'. Among the more robust, upright, and tallest of the variants, with small slender leaves providing an appealing contrast.

Thamnocalamus nepalensis

Height: 5–10 ft. (1.5–3 m)
Diameter: ½ in. (1.25 cm) max.
Light: partial shade
Zone 8

One of the more recently recognized Himalayan *Thamnocalamus* species, this bamboo is native to Nepal and Tibet. The culm leaves are hairless and the leaf sheaths have no fimbriae.

'**Nyalam**'. Upright in form. Shorter with larger leaves than other Himalayan bamboos of the genus and a less delicate appearance. New culm leaves have a striking red blush. Collected near Nyalam, Tibet, at an elevation of 11,900 ft. (3630 m).

Thamnocalamus crassinodus 'Merlyn'

Thamnocalamus nepalensis 'Nyalam'

Thamnocalamus tessellatus

Thamnocalamus tessellatus
Bergbamboes
Height: 10–20 ft. (3–6 m)
Diameter: 1 1/4 in. (3.2 cm) max.
Light: mostly sunny
Zone 7

The only bamboo indigenous to South Africa, this species grows in many areas of the country, sometimes covering vast areas of land. It is known by the Afrikaans name, bergbamboes. A South African mountain, Bamboesberg, is named after the bamboo that covers it.

This mountain bamboo grows in open clumps, up to 10 ft. (3 m) tall in dry areas and 20 ft. (6 m) tall in moister areas. At one time, the culms were used in Zulu shields, and forest peoples used them for the shafts of arrows and spears.

The culm and branch leaves are a striking bright creamy white in the first season, but they persist and can look a bit dingy and tattered in subsequent seasons. The culms turn a deep green. If exposed to strong sunlight, they take on purple tones.

THYRSOSTACHYS
Thyrsostachys is a genus of Old World tropical bamboos with slender erect culms, persistent culm leaves, a pachymorph rhizome system, and a clumping habit. The foliage leaves are much smaller and delicate than is typical for arborescent tropical bamboos. There are two known species.

Thyrsostachys oliveri
Height: 25–40 ft. (7.6–12 m)
Diameter: 3 1/4 in. (8.3 cm) max.
Light: full sun
Zone 10

Native to Burma and northern Thailand, *Thyrsostachys oliveri* is cultivated in the Chinese provinces of Yunnan and Guangdong. It is a highly

Thamnocalamus tessellatus, displaying the striking white culm leaves on a new culm.

Thyrsostachys oliveri

Thyrsostachys siamensis, new small clump.

attractive ornamental with towering upright culms and tufts of foliage. The culms are used for poles, construction, and handicrafts, and the new shoots are suitable for the table.

Thyrsostachys siamensis

Height: 25–40 ft. (7.6–12 m)
Diameter: 3 in. (7.5 cm) max.
Light: full sun
Zone 10

This species is native to Thailand and Burma and cultivated in China's Yunnan Province. The foliage leaves are exceptionally delicate and slender, particularly for an arborescent tropical bamboo. Tightly spaced and upright, the culms create a narrow vertical column supporting great plumes of delicate foliage.

Often planted for its fine beauty, it is quite useful as well. The culms are thick walled but slender, and have a variety of uses, such as fishing poles, tools and construction, and as a source for paper pulp. New shoots are harvested for the table and for commercial processing.

YUSHANIA

Primarily consisting of temperate-climate, moderately hardy, shrublike mountain bamboos, *Yushania* species have pachymorph rhizomes. In their native environments, they are found at elevations of 6000 to 12,000 ft. (1800 to 3700 m), and sometimes form dense thickets that can prohibit trees or other vegetation from regenerating. The plants are often browsed heavily by livestock and other animals, so their maximum height may seldom be achieved in the wild.

Because the rhizome necks vary in length and some are elongated, *Yushania* species do not form dense clumps. Instead, they exhibit a slight to pronounced spreading habit. New rhizomes arising from the lower buds closer to the rhizome neck have long, rootless rhizome necks that may be more than a foot (30 cm) long. New rhizomes arising from the upper buds closer to the culm have shorter rhizome necks.

In succeeding years, this growth habit may produce small clumps spaced apart from other small clumps. Larger plants in optimized growing conditions exaggerate the spreading habit and behave like moderate runners. Smaller plants in less optimized conditions will exhibit more of a clumping habit.

Yushania alpinia

Height: 20–55 ft. (6–17 m)
Diameter: 5 in. (13 cm) max.
Light: full sun
Zone 9

Yushania alpinia is an unusual member of the genus from equatorial Africa, where it is found at elevations of 8000 to 10,000 ft. (2400 to 3000 m). In the 1940s and 1950s, much of the bamboo forest land was cleared to plant fast-growing, exotic, softwood trees. In spite of the loss, *Y. alpinia* still covers some 385,000 acres

Yushania alpinia, showing its prominent aerial roots on the culm nodes.

Yushania anceps

(156,000 hectares) in Kenya. These bamboo forests are habitat for elephants and buffalo, as well as a food source for monkeys. The culms are used by the local peoples for water pipes, furniture, weaving, crafts, and construction. Unfortunately, *Yushania alpinia* grows well only in a narrow range of conditions, and prospers in few places outside of its native African environment.

Yushania anceps

Height: 8–25 ft. (2.4–7.6 m)
Diameter: ¾ in. (2 cm) max.
Light: partial shade
Zone 8
Native to India, *Yushania anceps* was introduced into Britain in 1865 and is the most well known example of the genus in the Western world. In its native India, it is distributed primarily in cool temperate to subalpine climate zones. At one time, this species reportedly formed dense undergrowth covering more than 50 square miles (130 square kilometers) in one area of India.

The culms are traditionally used to weave baskets and mats. The primary form has a maximum height about half what is cited here.

'Pitt White'. From the gardens at Pitt White in England. Narrower leaves and much larger in stature than the primary form. A popular bamboo in England.

Yushania boliana

Height: 12–24 ft. (4–7.3 m)
Diameter: 2 in. (5 cm) max.
Light: partial shade
Zone 7
From Sichuan, China, *Yushania boliana* is a robust, vigorous, attractive montane bamboo. The new culms are bright pale blue-green, sometimes

Yushania anceps 'Pitt White'

Yushania boliana

turning reddish purple with age. For a time its identity was something of a mystery, and it has been in circulation in the nursery trade as *Himalayacalamus intermedius* and *Borinda boliana*. It has an open clumping habit, particularly when grown in warmer conditions, but for a large and robust *Yushania* it spreads modestly.

Yushania brevipaniculata

Height: 4–8 ft. (1.2–2.4 m)
Diameter: ³⁄₄ in. (1 cm) max.
Light: partial shade
Zone 6

Yushania brevipaniculata comes from western Sichuan, China, at an elevation range of 5900 to 12,500 ft. (1770 to 3800 m). One of the smaller *Yushania*, it is among the hardiest of the genus. The native habitat encompasses a broad spectrum, from riverbanks and valley floors to steep slopes and various spruce, pine, oak, and beech

forests. Although widespread in pine forests where soils are typically acidic, it is also reportedly tolerant of alkaline soils. Frequently an understory shrub, it grows even more vigorously in openings in the forest canopy.

Auricles and fimbriae on the culm leaves are exceptionally large. New shoots are edible. It is a major food source for the giant panda.

Yushania exilis

Height: 5–10 ft. (1.5–3 m)
Diameter: ³⁄₈ in. (1 cm) max.
Light: partial shade
Zone 7

Yushania exilis comes from southern Sichuan, China, at an elevation range of 4000 to 5000 ft. (1200 to 1500 m). It is a smaller example of the genus, somewhat resembling *Y. brevipaniculata* but inhabiting the understory at lower elevations. It is small-leaved and attractive.

Yushania brevipaniculata, showing exaggerated auricles and fimbriae.

Yushania exilis

Yushania maculata

Yushania maling

Yushania maculata

Height: 5–10 ft. (1.5–3 m)
Diameter: ⅝ in. (1.5 cm) max.
Light: partial shade
Zone 6

Yushania maculata is an understory plant from the pine forests of northeastern Yunnan and southwestern Sichuan Provinces, China, at elevations of 6000 to 11,500 ft. (1800 to 3500 m). A recent introduction to the United States, it is among the more attractive bamboos of the genus. The dark culm sheaths contrast with the bluish gray new culms. Long, slender leaves add to the appeal.

Yushania maling

Height: 10–30 ft. (3–9 m)
Diameter: 2 in. (5 cm) max.
Light: mostly sunny
Zone 7

The most common temperate bamboo in eastern Nepal, *Yushania maling* is also native to Sikkim, West Bengal, and western Bhutan. It is often a dominant plant in the forest understory, forming dense thickets.

In cultivation it is typically much shorter than the cited maximum height. The shoots are suitable for the table. The leaves are used for animal fodder. Although not ideal, the culms are sometimes used to make baskets and fences.

This reasonably attractive bamboo can look scruffy if growing conditions are not ideal. Other members of the genus are often better choices for the landscape.

NURSERY SOURCES

This is a partial list of retail bamboo nurseries that are either open to the public with regular business hours, or else offer mail order, or both. Prior to visiting any nursery, it is recommended that you either call ahead or check the nursery's website for business hours and plants and services offered. This list is limited to nurseries in Canada, the United States, Scotland, England, and Ireland. Catalogs or lists are available from most.

No endorsement is intended, nor is criticism implied of sources not mentioned. More extensive listings of bamboo sources, including those that offer only local sales or visits by appointment only, are available through the American Bamboo Society at www.americanbamboo.org/SpeciesSourceList-Pages/PlantAndProductSources.html, and through individual country links on the European Bamboo Society's website at http://www.bamboosociety.org.

Canada

Canada's Bamboo World
8450 Banford Road
Chilliwack, BC V2P 6H3
604-792-9003
www.bambooworld.com

The Plant Farm
177 Vesuvius Bay Road
Salt Spring Island, BC V8K 1K3
250-537-5995
www.theplantfarm.ca

England

Abbotsbury Sub Tropical Gardens
Abbotsbury, Weymouth
Dorset DT3 4LA
01305 871344
www.abbotsburyplantsales.co.uk

Drysdale Garden Exotics
Bowerwood Road, Fordingbridge
Hampshire SP6 1BN
01425 653010

Fulbrooke Nursery
Home Farm, Westley Waterless
Newmarket CB8 0RG
01638 507124
www.fulbrooke.co.uk

Jungle Giants
Ferney Nurseries
Onibury SY7 9BJ
01584 856200
www.junglegiants.co.uk

Pan-Global Plants
The Walled Garden
Frampton on Severn
Gloucestershire GL2 7EX
01452 741641
www.panglobalplants.com

PW Plants
Sunnyside
Heath Road, Kenninghall
Norfolk NR16 2DS
01953 888212
www.hardybamboo.com

The Rodings Plantery
Anchor Lane, Abbess Roading
Essex CM5 0JP
07790 020940
www.therodingsplantery.co.uk

Whitelea Nursery
Whitelea Lane
Tansley, Matlock
Derbyshire DE4 5FL
01629 55010
www.uk-bamboos.co.uk

Ireland

Stam's Nurseries
The Garden House
Cappoquin, County Waterford
353 58 54787

Scotland

Scottish Bamboo Nursery
Middlemuir Farm
Craigievar, Alford
Aberdeenshire AB33 8JS
019755 81316

United States

A Bamboo Gardener
P.O. Box 17949
Seattle, WA 98127
206-371-1072
www.bamboogardener.com

A Bamboo Man
7810 SW 118 Street
Miami, FL 33156
305-378-9449
http://www.bambooman.net

Alligator Alley
4636 NW 10th Street
Oklahoma City, OK 73127
405-949-2553
www.alligatoralley.com/bamboostock.html

Bamboo Collection
9700 SW 114 Street
Miami, FL 33176
305-205-8184

Bamboo Company Nursery
16483 Fisher Road
Franklinton, LA 70438
985-789-2584
www.moso.us

Bamboo Garden
18900 NW Collins Road
North Plains, OR 97133
503-647-2700
www.bamboogarden.com

Bamboo Gardens of Louisiana
38124 Highway 440
Mount Hermon, LA 70450
985-795-2300
www.bamboogardensla.com

Bamboo Giant
5601 Freedom Blvd.
Aptos, CA 95003
831-687-0100
www.bamboogiant.com

Bamboo Guy Nursery
P.O. Box 357
Beaver, OR 97108
503-842-7329
www.bambooguy.com

Bamboo Headquarters
2498 Majella Road
Vista, CA 92084
760-758-6181
www.bambooheadquarters.com

Bamboo & Koi Garden
2115 SW Borland Road
West Linn, OR 97068
503-638-0888

Bamboo Plantation
642 Columbine Lane SW
Brookhaven, MS 39601
601-833-3937
www.bambooplantation.com

Bamboo Ranch
Tucson, AZ 85745
520-743-9879
www.bambooranch.net

Bamboo Sourcery
666 Wagnon Road
Sebastopol, CA 95472
707-823-5866
www.bamboosourcery.com

Bambu-u
2760 Gibbs Lake Road
Chimacum, WA 98325
360-531-0804
www.bambu-u.com

Bastian's Bamboo
2812 140th Ave SW
Tenino, WA 98589
360-357-7299

BeautifulBamboo.com
19546 Bamboo Bend Drive
Groveland, FL 34736
352-429-2425
www.beautifulbamboo.com

Beauty & The Bamboo
306-NW. 84th St.
Seattle, WA 98117
206-781-9790

Bountiful Earth
1200 West Canal Street
New Smyrna Beach, FL 32168
386-427-3330
www.bamboo.ws

Boxhill Farm
14175 Carnation-Duvall Road
Duvall, WA 98019
425-788-6473
www.boxhillfarm.com

Burt Associates Bamboo
3 Landmark Road
Westford, MA 01886
978-692-3240
www.bamboos.com

Burton's Bamboo Garden
7352 Gheils Carroll Road
Morrow, OH 45152
877-899-3446
www.burtonsbamboogarden.com

Caldwell Nursery & Botanic Garden
2436 Band Road
Rosenberg, TX 77471
281-342-4016
www.caldwellhort.com

Clinton Bamboo Growers
12260 1st Avenue South
Seattle, WA 98168
206-242-8848

Connor Bamboo
Portland, OR 97211
503-734-5735
www.connorbamboo.com

David C Andrews
P.O. Box 358
Oxon Hill, MD 20750

Dunroven Farm
7423 County Road 247
Rutland, FL 33538
352-330-0766
www.kingsbamboo.com

Gaia Yoga Nursery
RR2 #3334
Pahoa, HI 96778
808-965-5664
www.gaiayoga.org/nursery

Halfside Bamboo
161 SE Currie Way
Shelton, WA 98584
360-432-8493
www.halfsidebamboo.com

Healing Garden & Bamboo
9299 County Line Road
Spring Hill, FL 34608
352-428-3330
www.healinggardenandbamboo.com

Horseshoe Nursery
22 Hanson Drive
Horseshoe Bend, ID 83629
208-793-4121
www.horseshoenursery.com

Jade Mountain Bamboo Nursery
5020 116th Street East
Tacoma, WA 98446
253-548-1129
www.jademountainbamboo.com

jmbamboo
4176 Humber Road
Dora, AL 35062
205-283-5638
www.jmbamboo.com

Johnson Bamboo
70 Lark Avenue
Brooksville, FL 34601
352-544-0330
www.johnsonbamboo.com

Lewis Bamboo
121 Creekview Road
Oakman, AL 35579
205-686-5728
www.lewisbamboo.com

Little Acre Farm
223 Victory Road
Howell, NJ 07731
732-938-6300
www.littleacrebamboo.com

Lone Oak Farm
2219 Neely's Bend Road
Madison, TN 37115
615-865-9933
www.loneoakfarm-bamboo.com

McKenzie Valley Bamboo
38753 Camp Creek Road
Springfield, OR 97478
541-746-9734
www.mckenziebamboo.com

Michigan Bamboo Company
1016 Woodsboro
Royal Oak, MI 48067
248-298-9568
www.mibamboo.com

MidAtlantic Bamboo
1458 Dusty Road
Crewe, VA 23930
434-645-7662
www.midatlanticbamboo.com

Needmore Bamboo Company
Nashville, IN 47448
812-988-6896
www.needmorebamboo.com

New England Bamboo Company
5 Granite Street
Rockport, MA 01966
978-546-3581
www.newengbamboo.com

Porter Swamp Company
P.O. Box 491
Chadbourn, NC 28431
910-654-4628
www.porterswamp.com

Quindembo Bamboo Nursery
62-2182 O'uli Street
Kamuela, HI 96743
808-885-4968
www.bamboonursery.com

River's End Nursery and Farm
Box 1729
Los Fresnos, TX 78566
956-233-4792
www.riversendnursery.com

Shweeash Bamboo
Seaside, OR
503-440-2998
www.shweeashbamboo.com

Steve Ray's Bamboo Gardens
250 Cedar Cliff Road
Springville, AL 35146
205-594-3438
www.thebamboogardens.com

Touch the Earth
54 Georgian Road
Morristown, NJ 07960
973-538-2218
www.idigbamboo.com

Tradewinds Bamboo Nursery
28446 Hunter Creek Loop
Gold Beach, OR 97444
541-247-0835
www.bamboodirect.com

Tripple Brook Farm
37 Middle Road
Southampton, MA 01073
413-527-4626
www.tripplebrookfarm.com

Tropical Bamboo
2929 G Road East
Loxahatchee, FL 33470
954-461-7572
www.tropicalbamboo.com

Upper Bank Nurseries
PO Box 486
Media, PA 19063
610-566-0679

Viewcrest Nurseries
12713 NE 184th Street
Battle Ground, WA 98604
360-687-5167
www.viewcrest.com

Whispering Winds Bamboo
HRC1, Box 180
Hana, HI 96713
808-248-7561
www.whisperingwindsbamboo.com

Young Bamboo
1304 SW 202nd Street
Newberry, FL 32669
352-472-1359
www.youngbamboo.com

Zone 9 Tropicals
1015 Arlington Street
Houston, TX 77008
713-863-0708
www.zone9tropicals.com

GLOSSARY

aerial root a root growing above ground level. Some bamboos have a tendency to produce aerial roots at their culm and branch nodes.

arborescent having the form and characteristics of a tree; treelike. The large timber bamboos are arborescent.

auricle the earlike flaps that extend from the upper part of a sheath on both sides of the blade. Depending on the species, auricles may be prominent or entirely lacking. Regardless of species, auricles are entirely absent from rhizome sheaths.

axis a central stem along which plant parts are arrayed.

bamboos grasses of the subfamily Bambusoideae. The woody species of the subfamily belong to the tribe Bambuseae. The herbaceous species belong to the tribe Olyreae.

blade the part of the leaf that is typically flat and green and is dedicated to photosynthetic activity. On a culm leaf, the blade is very small compared to the sheath. On a foliage leaf the blade is very large compared to the sheath.

bud a small, dormant protuberance on a stem or branch, from which a shoot, leaf, or flower may arise. In bamboo, the buds on rhizomes can produce a culm or other rhizomes. Buds on culms and branches can produce branches or leaves.

clumping tightly grouped or clumped. Bamboos with short-necked, pachymorph rhizomes have a clumping habit. Bamboos that normally have a running habit may sometimes display more of a clumping habit if grown in cooler or shadier conditions than their norm.

culm an aboveground stem on a grass plant. The term is commonly associated with bamboo. Relative to other grass plants, the culms of most bamboos are very large and woody.

culm leaf a large, overlapping leaf that encases an emerging culm, protecting it and providing temporary support while it lignifies. The sheath portion of the culm leaf is far larger than the blade. In common terminology the culm leaf is sometimes called the "culm sheath." See also *foliage leaf*.

culm sheath see *culm leaf*.

deciduous shedding or falling away at a specific season or period of growth. Culm leaves, for example, may be deciduous or may be persistent.

fimbriae bristly, fringelike hairs that extend from the margins of the leaf sheath, usually from the auricles. They range from prominent to entirely lacking, depending on the species.

foliage leaf the type of leaf that is responsible for nearly all of the bamboo plant's photosynthetic activity. To this end, the blade is the predominant part of the foliage leaf, whereas the sheath is typically much smaller and is scarcely apparent on casual observation. See also *culm leaf*.

gregarious flowering the simultaneous flowering of a given generation of bamboo. The flowering is termed gregarious when most or all of the same bamboo generation begin flowering.

herbaceous not woody; having no persistent aerial parts. Virtually all of our familiar bamboos are woody, but many less well-known bamboo species are herbaceous.

inflorescence a flower cluster. Inflorescences have distinctive characteristics that help define genera, and in spite of other tools now available, they continue to play an important role in bamboo taxonomy.

internode the part of the culm between two nodes.

leaf the primary photosynthetic organ. Most, but not all, leaves have a photosynthetic function. In the context of bamboos and other grasses, the sheath and blade are the primary parts of the leaf. All bamboos and other grasses have foliage leaves; woody bamboos have culm leaves as well.

leptomorph a type of rhizome that typically runs laterally and does not turn upward to become a culm—although a leptomorph rhizome can under some circumstances become a culm. A leptomorph rhizome is usually hollow and smaller in diameter than the culms that originate from it. The rhizome neck is always short. Internodes are longer than wide. Nodes are sometimes prominent. Buds are arranged horizontally. Most buds remain dormant, but those that germinate may produce either culms or new rhizomes. Bamboo species with leptomorph rhizome systems are commonly associated with running bamboos.

montane of, or growing in, mountainous areas.

neck usually associated with the rhizome, the neck is a structural element of every segmented axis of the bamboo plant, including the culm, branches, and rhizome. Structurally, the neck permits creation of a new and larger axis. The highly compressed stacking of progressively larger internodes can create a new axis much larger than the axis from which it originated. This is well illustrated by the rhizomes and culms of leptomorph timber bamboos. The rhizomes are proportionally much smaller in diameter than the culms (new axes) they generate. The highly compressed internodes of the neck progressively increase in diameter to form the base of the culm.

node the point on a culm, branch, or other axis where leaves, shoots, branches, roots, or flowers are attached. In the context of bamboo, the nodes delimit the segments of the segmented structure.

pachymorph a type of rhizome that always turns upward and becomes a culm. It is nearly always curved and, at its maximum width, is slightly thicker than the aboveground culm it becomes. Rhizome nodes are not prominent. The internodes are wider than long, and usually solid. New rhizomes emerge from lateral buds on an existing rhizome. As with the original rhizome, these new rhizomes always turn upward and become culms. The neck of the rhizome can be either long or short. This rhizome structure is commonly associated with clumping bamboos. Some species with pachymorph rhizome systems do not exhibit a clumping habit. Most of these are tropical bamboos that are not in cultivation in most of North America or Europe.

palmate three or more leaves or leaflets originating from an apparent common point, in the manner of a palm.

persistent not deciduous; not shedding or falling away. Culm leaves, for example, may be persistent or may be deciduous.

propagule a new plant created from a parent plant.

pubescent covered with short, fine hairs.

rhizome an underground stem, or underground portion of a stem. The rhizome has the same or similar structure as the culm, the aboveground stem. It has nodes, internodes, leaves (here generally consisting of the sheath with no blade), and roots.

root the (usually) underground part of a plant that absorbs water and nutrients. It also serves to anchor the plant in the soil. It is the only bamboo axis that does not have a segmented structure—that is, unlike culms, branches, and rhizomes, roots have no nodes, internodes, or leaves.

running widely spaced; culms arising far apart and usually singly rather than in groups. Bamboos with leptomorph rhizomes typically have a running habit. Some bamboos with long-necked pachymorph rhizomes may also have a running habit, but most of these are tropical bamboos not in cultivation in most of North America or Europe. See *clumping*.

sheath the lower part of the leaf that tightly encircles the stem or branch. In bamboo. it is a very large and prominent part of the culm leaf, but a much smaller, and sometimes barely noticeable, part of the foliage leaf. See also *blade.*

sheath scar a mark left around the lowermost part of the node where the sheath was attached.

sport a plant that is markedly different from the parent plant, generally as the result of a mutation.

sulcus a pronounced groove running the length of the internode, caused by the presence of a developing branch bud at the internode's base, grooving the culm as the internode elongates. A prominent sulcus is a distinguishing characteristic of the genus *Phyllostachys.*

taxon (pl. **taxa**) a taxonomic category or group.

tessellation fine cross-veining in leaves, creating a gridlike or checkered appearance that is visible on close examination. Not all bamboo leaves are tessellated. Tessellation is associated with greater cold hardiness. Most or all tropical bamboos have no leaf tessellation.

thorn a stiff, woody, modified branch that ends in a sharp point. Some tropical and semitropical bamboo species have thorns.

tillering sending forth new shoots from the base of a stem. In the context of bamboos, tillering refers to new culms that arise from the basal buds of existing culms without an intervening rhizome. It is characteristic of some bamboo species with leptomorph rhizome systems. Although sometimes superficially similar, bamboos with pachymorph rhizome systems are not tillering, per se, but rather have an intervening (though unified) rhizome between the existing stem and new culm.

woody lignified, not herbaceous; having persistent aerial parts. Bamboo does not have true wood, which is derived from secondary growth. Virtually all of our familiar bamboos are woody, but many, less well-known bamboo species are herbaceous.

FURTHER READING

Bell, M. 2000. *The Gardener's Guide to Growing Temperate Bamboos*. Portland, Oregon: Timber Press; Newton Abbot, Devon: David and Charles.

Crompton, D. 2006. *Ornamental Bamboos*. Portland, Oregon: Timber Press.

Cusack, V. 1999. *Bamboo World: The Growing and Use of Clumping Bamboos*. East Roseville, Australia: Kangaroo Press.

Farrelly, D. 1984. *The Book of Bamboo*. San Francisco, California: Sierra Club Books.

Judziewicz, E. J., L. G. Clark, X. Londoño, and M. J. Stern. 1999. *American Bamboos*. Washington, D.C.: Smithsonian Institution Press.

Lewis, D., and C. Miles. 2007. *Farming Bamboo*. Lulu.com.

McClure, F. A. 1966. *The Bamboos*. Cambridge, Massachusetts: Harvard University Press. Reprint. Washington, D.C.: Smithsonian Institution Press, 1993.

Meredith, T. J. 2001. *Bamboo for Gardens*. Portland, Oregon: Timber Press.

Stapleton, C. M. A. 1994. *The Bamboos of Bhutan*. Kew, England: The Royal Botanic Gardens.

Stapleton, C. M. A. 1994. *The Bamboos of Nepal*. Kew, England: The Royal Botanic Gardens.

Stapleton, C. M. A., B. Hollenback, and T. J. Meredith, eds. 2008. *Bamboo Species Source List*. Encinitas, California: American Bamboo Society.

Whittaker, P. 2005. *Hardy Bamboos: Taming the Dragon*. Portland, Oregon: Timber Press.

INDEX

Bold-faced numbers indicate photo pages.

arrow bamboo, 160, 162
Arundinaria, 33
Arundinaria funghomii, **33**
Arundinaria gigantea, 28, 30, 33, **34**
  'Macon', 34
Arundinaria pygmaea, 155
Arundinaria tecta, 30, **34**

Bambusa, 35, 77, 90, 92
Bambusa bambos, **35**, 36
Bambusa beecheyana, 29, 31, **36**, 37
  var. *pubescens*, 37
Bambusa chungii, **37**
  var. *barbelatta*, 37
Bambusa dolichoclada 'Stripe', 31, **37**, 39
Bambusa dolichomerithalla, 39
  'Green Stripestem', 39
  'Silverstripe', **38**, 39
Bambusa eutuldoides, 39
  'Viridivittata', 31, **39**
Bambusa lako, 29, 31, **39**, 40, 91
Bambusa malingensis, 29, **40**
Bambusa membranacea, 29, 30–31, **40–41**
Bambusa multiplex, 28–29, 31, 40, 45
  'Alphonse Karr', **42**
  'Fernleaf', 31, **42**
  'Fernleaf Stripestem', 31, 42, **43**
  'Golden Goddess', 42
  'Goldstripe', 42
  'Midori Green', 42
  'Riviereorum', 29, 31, 42, **44**
  'Silverstripe', 28, **44**
  'Tiny Fern', 29, **45**
  'Tiny Fern Striped', 45
  'Willowy', 45
Bambusa nana (hort.), **44**, 45
Bambusa oldhamii, 29, 31, **45**
Bambusa pachinensis, 31, **46**
Bambusa pygmaea, 155
Bambusa textilis, 29–31, 45, **46–47**
  var. *albostriata*, 46
  'Dwarf', 46
  var. *glabra*, 46
  var. *gracilis*, 46
  'Kanapaha', 48

'Maculata', 48
'Mutabilis', 48
'Scranton', 48
Bambusa tuldoides, 29, **48**
Bambusa ventricosa, **48**
  'Kimmei', **49**
Bambusa vulgaris, 29, 31, 35, **49**
  'Vittata', 28, 29, 49, **50**
  'Wamin', 29, 50
  'Wamin Striata', 29, **50**
Bashania, 50
Bashania fargesii, 30, **50**, 51
Beechey bamboo, 37
bergbamboes, 187
black bamboo, 134
blowpipe bamboo, 39
blue bamboo, 96
Borinda, 51, 84
Borinda albocerea, **51**
Borinda angustissima, 27–28, 51, **52**
Borinda boliana, 192
Borinda contracta, 28, **53**
Borinda fungosa, 27–30, **53**, 55
  'White Cloud', 55
Borinda lushuiensis, 28–29, **54**, 55
Borinda macclureana, 29, **55–56**, 57
Borinda nujiangensis, **57**
Borinda papyrifera, 28–29, **57**
Borinda perlonga, **58**
Borinda sp. 'KR 5288', 58, **59**
Borinda sp. 'Muliensis', **58**
Borinda yulongshanensis, 58, **60**
Buddha's belly bamboo, 48–49

candy-stripe bamboo, 96
canebrake bamboo, 33
Cephalostachyum, 60
Cephalostachyum pergracile, **60**
Chimonobambusa, 20, 60–61
Chimonobambusa macrophylla 'Intermedia', **61**
Chimonobambusa marmorea, 28–30, 61, **62**
  'Variegata', **62**
Chimonobambusa quadrangularis, 28–29, **61**, 62
  'Joseph de Jussieu', 63
  'Suow', **62**, 63
  'Yellow Groove', **62**, 63

Chimonobambusa tumidissinoda, 27, 29, 61, **63**
Chimonocalamus, 63
Chimonocalamus pallens, **64**
Chinese goddess bamboo, 42
Chinese temple bamboo, 183
Chinese walking stick bamboo, 63
Chusquea, 22, 64
Chusquea acuminata, 77
Chusquea andina, **65**
Chusquea breviglumis, 72
Chusquea circinata, **65**
  'Chiapas', 67
Chusquea coronalis, **66**, 65, 67
Chusquea culeou, 27–28, 30, 65, **67**, 72, 77
  'Argentina', **69**
  'Caña Prieta', 27–28, 30, **69**
  'Hillier', **68**, 69
Chusquea cumingii, 28, 30, **69–70**
Chusquea delicatula, 28, **70**
Chusquea foliosa, 70, **71**, 75, 77
Chusquea gigantea, 27, **72**
Chusquea glauca, 72, **73**
Chusquea liebmannii, **73**
Chusquea mimosa subsp. *australis*, **73**
Chusquea pittieri, 28, **74**, 75
Chusquea sp. 'Chiconquiaco', **74**, 75
Chusquea sp. 'Las Vigas', **75**
Chusquea subtilis, **75**, 77
Chusquea tenuis, **76**, 77
Chusquea tomentosa, 28, **76**, 77
Chusquea uliginosa, 30, **76**, 77
Chusquea valdiviensis, **76**, 77

Dendrocalamus, **77**
Dendrocalamus asper, 29–31, **77**
  'Betung Hitam', 78
  'Nubian Queen', **78**
Dendrocalamus brandisii, 29, **78**
  'Black', 79
  Variegated, 79
Dendrocalamus giganteus, **12**, 29–31, **79**
  Variegated, 79
Dendrocalamus hamiltonii, 29, **80**
Dendrocalamus latiflorus, 29, 31, 80
  'Mei-nung', **80**
Dendrocalamus membranaceus, 40
Dendrocalamus minor, 80, **81**
  'Amoenus', 80
Dendrocalamus strictus, **82**, 77
Drepanostachyum, 82, 96

Drepanostachyum falcatum, 97
Drepanostachyum hookerianum, 96
Drepanostachyum khasianum, 82, **83**
dwarf fernleaf, 151
dwarf whitestripe, 153

Fargesia, 9–10, 22, **23**, 51, 84–86, 184–185
Fargesia apicirubens, 28, **84–85**
  'White Dragon', **84**, 85
Fargesia denudata, 28, **85**
Fargesia dracocephala, 85
  'Rufa', 28, 85, **86**
Fargesia murielae, 27–28, 84–85, **86**, 88
Fargesia nitida, **12**, 27–28, 84, 86, **88**
  'Juizhaigou', **88**
  'Nymphenburg', **87**, 88
Fargesia robusta, 27–29, **88**, 89
  'Campbell', 89
  'Wolong', **89**
Fargesia sp. 'Scabrida', **2**, 27, 29, **89**
Fargesia utilis, 89, **90**
fishpole bamboo, 111
fountain bamboo, 86

giant thorny bamboo, 35
giant timber bamboo, 45
Gigantochloa, 90
Gigantochloa apus, **91**
Gigantochloa atroviolacea, 30–31, 40, **91**
Gigantochloa pseudoarundinacea, 31, 90–92, **93**
Gigantochloa verticillata, 92
golden bamboo, 111–112
gray bamboo, 64
Guadua, 92
Guadua aculeata, 92, **93**
Guadua amplexifolia, 92, **93**
Guadua angustifolia, 30–31, 92, **93**, 94
  'Bicolor', 94
  'Less Thorny', 94
Guadua paniculata, **94**

hedge bamboo, 40
Hibanobambusa, 94–95
Hibanobambusa tranquillans, 95
  'Shiroshima', 27–29, **95**
Himalayacalamus, 82, 95–96
Himalayacalamus asper, 97
Himalayacalamus falconeri, 96
  'Damarapa', **96**
Himalayacalamus hookerianus, 28–29, 96, **97**

Himalayacalamus intermedius, 192
Himalayacalamus planatus, **97–98**, 99
Himalayacalamus porcatus, **99**

incense bamboo, 108
Indian thorny bamboo, 35
Indocalamus, 100, 147
Indocalamus latifolius, 27, 30, **100**
Indocalamus sp. 'Hamadae', **101**
Indocalamus sp. 'Solidus', **101**
Indocalamus tessellatus, 27–28, 30, 101, **102**

Japanese timber bamboo, 116

leopard-skin bamboo, 136

madake, 116
male bamboo, 82
marbled bamboo, 61
medake, 157
moso, 92, 123, 130

Nastus, 102
Nastus elatus, **102**
Neomicrocalamus microphyllus, 97

Oldham's bamboo, 45
Olmeca, 103
Olmeca recta, **103**
Olmeca reflexa, 103
Otatea, 94, 103
Otatea acuminata, 28, 103
   subsp. *acuminata*, 103
   subsp. *aztecorum*, 30, 31, **104**
   subsp. *aztecorum* 'Dwarf', 104
   'Michoacán', **104**
Otatea fimbriata, **104**
Oxytenanthera, 105
Oxytenanthera braunii, **105**

Phyllostachys, 24, 33, 51, 94–95, 175–176,
   178, 183, 202
Phyllostachys angusta, 27, 29–30, **107–108**
Phyllostachys arcana, **108**
   'Luteosulcata', 108, **109**
Phyllostachys atrovaginata, **8**, 9, 27–30, 108,
   110
Phyllostachys aurea, 27–30, 107, **111**, 132
   'Albovariegata', 112
   'Dr. Don', **111**,
   'Flavescens-Inversa', **112**
   'Holochrysa', **112**

'Koi', **112**
'Takemurai', 113
Phyllostachys aureosulcata, 18, 27–29, **113**,
   119, 123
   'Alata', **113**
   'Aureocaulis', 113, **114**
   'Harbin', **115**
   'Harbin Inversa', **115**
   'Pekinensis', 115
   'Spectabilis', **115**
Phyllostachys bambusoides, 19, 27–30, 107,
   116–117, 124, 137, 145
   'Albovariegata', **118**
   'Allgold', 29, **118**
   'Castillon', 29, **118**
   'Castillon Inversa',
   'Golden Dwarf', 118
   'Job's Spots', 118
   'Kawadana', 29, **119**
   'Marliac', **119**
   'Ribleaf', 119
   'Richard Haubrich', 119, **120–121**
   'Slender Crookstem', 119
   'Subvariegata', 121
   'White Crookstem', 121
Phyllostachys bissetii, 18, 27–30, 107, **121**
   'Dwarf', 123
Phyllostachys dulcis, **13**, **21**, 29–30, **122–123**
Phyllostachys edulis, 19, 27, 29–30, 107, 116,
   123–125, 126, 130, 137
   'Anderson', 126
   'Bicolor', 126
   'Goldstripe', **126**
   'Heterocycla', **126**
Phyllostachys flexuosa, 30, **127**
   'Kimmei', 127
   'Spring Beauty', **127**
Phyllostachys glauca, 29–30, 127, **128**
   'Notso', 128
   'Yunzhu', **128**
Phyllostachys heteroclada, 27, 29–30, 108,
   128, **129**
   'Purpurata', 128
   'Solidstem', 128
Phyllostachys heterocycla f. *pubescens*, 123
Phyllostachys humilis, 27, 29–30, 105, 28, **129**
Phyllostachys iridescens, 27, 30, 129, **130**
Phyllostachys kwangsiensis, **130**
Phyllostachys lithophila, 130, **131**
Phyllostachys makinoi, 27, 29–30, 132, **133**
Phyllostachys mannii, 27–30, 132
   'Decora', 132, **133**

Phyllostachys meyeri, 30, 132, **133**
Phyllostachys nidularia, 27, 29–30, 132, **133**
  'Farcta', 132
  'June Barbara', 132
  'Smoothsheath', 132
Phyllostachys nigra, 19–20, 27, 29–30, **134**, 136
  'Bory', 27, 29–30, **136**, 137
  'Daikokuchiku', 136
  'Hale', **135**, 136
  'Henon',18, 27, 29–30, 116, 124, 136, **137**
  'Megurochiku', 27, 29, **136**, 137
  'Mejiro', 137
  'Muchisasa', 137
  'Othello', 137
  'Punctata', 137
  'Shimadake', 137
  'Tosaensis', 137
Phyllostachys nuda, 27–30, 107, 123, **138**
  'Localis', 138
Phyllostachys parvifolia, 138, **139**
Phyllostachys platyglossa, 27, 30, **138**
Phyllostachys praecox, 27, 30, 140
  'Prevernalis', **140**
  'Viridisulcata', **140**
Phyllostachys propinqua, 140
  'Beijing', 140, **141**
Phyllostachys rubromarginata, 28, 30, **141**
Phyllostachys stimulosa, **142**
Phyllostachys violascens, 107, **142**
Phyllostachys viridis, 27, 29–30, 107, 132, 143
  'Houzeau', **143**
  'Robert Young', **9–10**, 143
Phyllostachys vivax, **6**, 7, 20, 27–30, **32**, 33,
    116, 124, **144–145**, 147
  'Aureocaulis', **145–146**, 147
  'Huangwenzhu', **145**, 147
  'Huangwenzhu Inversa', **147**
Pleioblastus, 147, 175, 182
Pleioblastus akebono, 27–29, **148**
Pleioblastus amarus, **148**
Pleioblastus argenteostriatus, 28, **149**
Pleioblastus chino, 29–30, **149**, 151
  'Angustifolia', 151
  'Elegantissimus', 151
  'Kimmei', 28, **151**
  'Murakamianus', 28, **151**
  'Vaginatus Variegata', 28, 29, **150**, 151
Pleioblastus distichus, 27–30, 151, **152**, 153
  'Mini', 153
Pleioblastus fortunei, 27–30, **152**, 153
Pleioblastus gramineus, 30, **152**, 153–154
  'Monstrispiralis', 153

Pleioblastus hindsii, 30, **153**
Pleioblastus kongosanensis, 154
  'Akibensis', 154
  'Aureostriatus', **154**
Pleioblastus linearis, 30, 154, **155**
  'Nana', 154
Pleioblastus pygmaeus, **9**, 27–30, 154, **155**,
    163
  'Ramosissimus', 155
Pleioblastus shibuyanus 'Tsuboi', 27–29, 155,
    156
Pleioblastus simonii, 29–30, **157**
  'Variegatus', **157**
Pleioblastus viridistriatus, 27–28, 30, **158**
  'Chrysophyllus', **159**
Pseudosasa, 158–159
Pseudosasa amabilis, **159**
Pseudosasa cantori, **160**
Pseudosasa japonica, 16, 27, 29–30, 160, **161**,
    162, 164
  'Akebono', **162**
  'Akebonosuji', **160**, 162–163
  'Pleioblastoides', 162
  'Tsutsumiana', 162
  'Variegata', 163
Pseudosasa longiligula, **162**, 163
Pseudosasa owatarii, 29, 158, **163**
Pseudosasa usawai, **163**
Pseudosasa viridula, **164**
punting pole bamboo, 48

Qiongzhuea tumidissinoda, 63

Raddia, 164
Raddia distichophylla, 28, **164**, 165
Rhipidocladum, 165
Rhipidocladum racemiflorum, **165**
river cane, 33

Sasa, 94–95, 100, 147, 165, **166–167**, 173–
    174
Sasa hayatae, **168**
Sasa kurilensis, 28, 168, **169**
  'Simofuri', 27–28, **168**, 169
Sasa nagimontana, 28, **169**
Sasa oshidensis, **170**
Sasa palmata, 27–28, 30, **171**
Sasa pygmaea, 155, 174
Sasa senanensis, 28, **171**
Sasa tsuboiana, 27–28, **172**
Sasa veitchii, 27–28, 168, **172**
  'Minor', 168

Sasaella, 147, 173
Sasaella masamuneana, 27–28, 30, 173
  'Albostriata', 28–29, **173**, 174
  'Aureostriata', 174
Sasaella ramosa, 27–29, **174**
Sasamorpha, 174
Sasamorpha borealis, **174**
Schizostachyum, 175
Schizostachyum brachycladum, **175**
  'Bali Kuning', 175
Semiarundinaria, 106, 175–176, 182–183
Semiarundinaria fastuosa, 27–30, **32**, 33, **176**,
  178–179
  'Viridis', 176
Semiarundinaria fortis, 27, 176, **177**
Semiarundinaria makinoi, 27, **178**
Semiarundinaria okuboi, 30, 178, **179**
Semiarundinaria yamadorii (hort.), 178
  'Brimscombe', 178, **179**
Semiarundinaria yashadake, 30, 178–179, **180**
  'Kimmei', **179**
Shibataea, 181
Shibataea chinensis, 28, **181**
Shibataea kumasaca, 27–30, 181, **182**
  'Albostriata', 182
  'Aureostriata', 182
Sinobambusa, 182–183
Sinobambusa intermedia, **183**
Sinobambusa tootsik, 183
  'Albostriata', 5, 28,**183**, 184
snakeskin bamboo, 136
square bamboo, 62
stone bamboo, 107
sweetshoot bamboo, 123
switch cane, 34

Thamnocalamus, 184
Thamnocalamus crassinodus, 27–28, 184–185
  'Aristatus', **12**, **184**, 185
  'Kew Beauty', 185
  'Mendocino', **184**, 185
  'Merlyn', **185**
Thamnocalamus nepalensis, 185
  'Nyalam', **185**
Thamnocalamus tessellatus, 28–29, 184,
  186–187
Thyrsostachys, 187
Thyrsostachys oliveri, 29, 31, **187**
Thyrsostachys siamensis, 29, **188**, 189
Taiwan stone bamboo, 130
tea stick bamboo, 159
tiger bamboo, 136
Timor Black, 39
Tonkin cane, 159
tortoise shell bamboo, 126

umbrella bamboo, 86

water bamboo, 128
weaver's bamboo, 46
windbreak bamboo, 50
wine bamboo, 105

yadake, 160
yellow groove bamboo, 113
Yushania, 13, 189
Yushania alpina, **189**, 181
Yushania anceps, 28–28, **190**, 191
  'Pitt White', **191**
Yushania boliana, 29, **191**, 192
Yushania brevipaniculata, 27–28, 30, **192**
Yushania exilis, **192**
Yushania maculata, **193**, 194
Yushania maling, **194**